THE "GROW or DIE" ULTIMATUM

DANIEL BORRIS

THE
"GROW or DIE"
ULTIMATUM

CREATING VALUE THROUGH ACQUISITION
AND BLENDED, LONG-TERM IMPROVEMENT

CRC Press
Taylor & Francis Group
Boca Raton   London   New York

CRC Press is an imprint of the
Taylor & Francis Group, an **informa** business

A PRODUCTIVITY PRESS BOOK

CRC Press
Taylor & Francis Group
6000 Broken Sound Parkway NW, Suite 300
Boca Raton, FL 33487-2742

Printed on acid-free paper
Version Date: 20160524

International Standard Book Number-13: 978-1-4987-5683-9 (Hardback)

Library of Congress Cataloging-in-Publication Data

Names: Borris, Daniel, author.
Title: The "grow or die" ultimatum : creating value through acquisition and
blended, long-term improvement formulas / Daniel Borris.
Description: Boca Raton, FL : Taylor & Francis, 2016.
Identifiers: LCCN 2016001965 | ISBN 9781498756839 (hardcover)
Subjects: LCSH: Consolidation and merger of corporations.
Classification: LCC HD2746.5 .B67 2016 | DDC 658.1/62--dc23
LC record available at https://lccn.loc.gov/2016001965

Visit the Taylor & Francis Web site at
http://www.taylorandfrancis.com

and the CRC Press Web site at
http://www.crcpress.com

Printed and bound in the United States of America by
Edwards Brothers Malloy on sustainably sourced paper

Contents

Preface

It seems to me that given the oft-quoted statistics regarding the high failure rate of acquired companies that achieve the targeted synergy savings, the synergies that triggered the acquisitions in the first place with some quotes as high as 95%, there is a need for a book on the topic that is largely aimed at medium-sized companies.

The main reasons for failure are often cited as including poor strategic fit, a failed cultural marriage, failure to identify crucial issues in the due diligence process, and failures resulting from any business integration. This book therefore is focused on this end of the M&A process. In addition, it highlights the need to ensure the current business is in optimum shape before adding a new one to the mix. Mergers and acquisitions are bloody hard work! It is unlikely that you would automate a production line before you had it working properly in a manual state. The same truth holds when grafting a new business onto an existing one.

Although the information in this book will prove of value to any company, I believe it is medium-sized businesses that likely need the most help. It is harder for them to recover from adverse financial surprises than it is for their larger sister companies, and yet often they are faced with the need to do an acquisition. They are unlikely to have a permanent M&A department or the financial resources to hire the top gun experts in the field and so they must make do with what they have. I sincerely hope the information in this book helps to fill that gap.

My brother Steven and I just had our book *The Success or Die Ultimatum* published by CRC Press, a publisher who is truly dedicated to supporting productivity across the globe. For me, this was my first book and for Steven his third. *The Success or Die Ultimatum* makes a very clear statement of how we feel about spreading our know-how and sharing what we believe works best. This follow-up book is intended to achieve those same goals with an expanded view on mergers and acquisitions.

Looking back at my life, it seems I remember almost everything; sometimes a casual statement can become a guiding principle. One guy told me that everything you ever learn in any job during your life goes into your briefcase and you carry it with you to the next job; nothing is ever lost. The years spent working on tool and die assist you when you are helping to turn around an automotive parts supplier in need; the experience you gain working as a shift manager in high-speed packaging helps when you're the COO of a plastics company. The analysis work you apply during a night-shift as a consultant in a call center makes you stronger when you are the managing director of a business process outsourcing company (BPO); truly nothing is ever lost.

My career has taken me across the globe, working as a senior executive and as a consultant and yet from the earliest days I was driven by the desire to simplify for others the learning that I gained along the way. To help achieve this in *The Success or Die Ultimatum*, we used a novel approach where we applied characterization to our cast of players as opposed to following a textbook approach. I have used the same style in these current writings, *The Grow or Die Ultimatum: Creating Value through Acquisition and Blended Long-Term Improvement Formulas*. The characters exhibit a conglomeration of traits I have encountered in real life but are not related to any specific people. The same holds true for the problems covered. In fact, more often than not the characters have been created as an amalgam of my own best and worst selves.

I hope you find it adds to your skill sets and that you enjoy reading it as much as I have enjoyed the writing of it.

Acknowledgments

I thank everyone at every level in every organization in which I have had the privilege to work. From the CEO to the frontline folks who keep their fingers on the green button and make the whole thing go every day, you are all heroes.

I'd also like to thank those who have mentored me along the way; there are many and I offer my apologies for naming only a few: George Ross, Elaine Minacs, John Crncich, and Brian Delaney.

My sincere gratitude is extended to Martin LaChapelle for the excellent graphic art work he has applied in taking my sketches and turning them into the 30 fine figures that illustrate this book.

I'd also like to thank Michael Sinocchi of Taylor & Francis Group for his help and support on the publication of this book and also on the publication of *The Succeed or Die Ultimatum*.

Finally, I thank my partner Becky for her love and encouragement during the writing of this book.

Introduction

See yourself as James the CEO of JKL Inc. It's a nice little business, not so little really at $1.5 billion per year in sales and 8% earnings before interest and taxes (EBIT). You pay your shareholders a nice steady dividend of 3% every year without exception and everyone is happy. The street views your stock as that of a value company, although your market cap also grows by 3% per year.

So why are you in the office on this bright and sunny Saturday morning at 7:00 a.m., and why are you pacing up and down, stop-starting and staring out the window?

This is exactly how your old friend John, the company COO, finds you; he is worried that you might be thinking about jumping!

You explain, "I'm fine, John, but we have to grow this business, as a conglomerate of four diverse divisions at approximately $375 million each in sales, we are a sitting duck for a hostile takeover. If it was best for all of our stakeholders, I wouldn't resist that, but I believe we can do better, and so, old friend, we must grow or die!"

"Who is pushing you on this?" asks John.

"No one," responds James. "I just feel it in my bones."

The four divisions represent food and beverage, metals distribution, automotive parts, and business process outsourcing (BPO) sectors. The overall corporation seems healthy, but the average performance hides harsh realities, which include recurring problems, a declining division, diverse cultures, underutilized capacity, poor morale, and fear.

The plan is to grow the top line of the business to $3.0 billion in five years and increase the overall profit margin by 50%. To achieve this, there will have to be at least one acquisition and it must be a success and there can't be any disappointments or disruption to our shareholders. But what's the point in making an acquisition if we can't run the current business effectively? What would the chance of success be?

So we will follow a parallel two-pronged approach: optimize the current business and search for the right acquisitions at the same time! We get it that we need help; our existing management will be stretched in fixing the current business, let alone growing it and integrating an acquisition. We should call someone we know and trust: Rory McGregor; he's helped us before!

Mergers and acquisitions are bloody hard work; you can't get better just by getting bigger! This book provides a guide through the steps involved in optimizing your current business in readiness to accept a new acquisition and covers acquisition criteria, including communications, establishing a high performance culture, selecting an M&A broker, strategic planning, project planning, screening the potential acquisitions, due diligence processing, business integration, team building, problem solving techniques, training the trainer, following the theory of constraints, and the ongoing management and control of the new expanded business entity.

All of the techniques introduced in this book can be used in any company and in any industry.

1

To Acquire or to Be Acquired

"So, James, what's the deal?"

I'm startled and I spin round: Who would be here at 7:00 on Saturday morning, other than me, that is? However, standing bold as brass in the doorway is my old friend John.

"What the hell are you doing here? Get home!" But John just laughs.

"Someone has to keep their eye on you, or you might jump out of that window instead of just staring out of it." John saunters into my office and sits on the couch. "And why are you here?" he demands.

"I couldn't sleep; you know that nagging feeling that you're missing something. You try to tell yourself that you don't know what it is, you don't want to admit it to yourself but deep down inside, you know?"

"Oh yes, I know that feeling very well, I knew you'd be here and that's why I'm here. So tell me, what's driving you crazy now?"

"It's Rory, John, I can't get him out of my head, if you know me as well as you say you do, then what's up with me now?"

"It seems to me that when you have a big new idea or when you're under pressure, you tend to look over your shoulder for Rory; you want to use him as a sounding board. It's a kind of what would Rory do, you know that!"

"But I have you, John, my old and trusty sidekick. Why can't I just bounce it off you as usual?"

"It must be big my friend, a little too big for the Lone Ranger and Tonto—it looks like you need a third mind. It's a little Alexandre Dumas maybe... but that's what it seems like to me."

"All these years and you still amaze me," I say. "Did you notice on your way in if the café was open downstairs yet?"

"It is. Joe's just setting up the tables, but he's got the coffee on though. Are you ready?"

"Sure, let's go down and I'll tell you what I'm thinking."

"I know what you're thinking."

"Impossible," I say, staring into my old friend's eyes.

"Regardless, you know I'm with you on it," says John, and we walk toward the elevator together.

We two have known each other for thirty years now. Back in the day, John was my boss, the plant manager in a high-speed packaging plant and I headed up training and development. He was all-knowing and all-annoying even then and I was ever keen to pick his brain; he said I was like a sponge, I think he meant it well.

All these years later we have had a change in the pecking order and now I'm the boss, but of course that's not really possible. It's like getting a bigger job than your dad and becoming the parent, you just can't do that. It's not as if John's my father; he just thinks he is!

Today, I play the role of CEO of a mid-size company with diverse business interests, and John plays the role of my number two, the COO. I swear the devil can read my mind!

Downstairs Joe says good morning and asks us if we ever sleep as he puts the coffees down in front of us. We both protest, but he is already walking back to the counter.

"You look a bit tired, Joe, you getting old?" John gibes. That gets Joe turn around with his wry look, but there's no comment. John sips his coffee.

I grab a few napkins and start to scribble out the plan, I hardly write a single word, just join up a few boxes with connecting arrows.

"Oh this will be fun," John mutters under his breath. "Merger and acquisition time again, is it?"

"I'm sorry," I say. "Why would you need to ask if you already know what I'm thinking?"

"Just a reflex action. Please continue, lord and master."

I swear sometimes I could kill him, but I refuse to show it. After all, John feels it's his role in life to bug me.

I fill in some of the boxes showing our various business interests and the related geography. I push in a few current financials, connect all the dependencies, and roll up our current gross sales and operating profits. I get this much on the back of one napkin and push it across the table to John. A couple of our employees arrive and give us a nod, they aren't at all surprised to see us sitting here together at 7:30 on a Saturday morning, in fact, they and just about any of our folks regardless of title would normally bring their coffee over and sit with us. But not today, they see we are busy and they respect that. God, I'm so happy we have this kind of relationship with our folks, sometimes I think we don't deserve it, but I guess overall we must have earned it.

John mulls over the work of art that is the first napkin and I'm already working on napkin number two. This time the boxes containing the elements of our business along with the financials show a required future state. I slide it over to John, he looks at it, and then he stares hard at me.

"It looks as if this business doubles in size from $1.5 billion to $3 billion. It doesn't trouble me though, you couldn't possibly have written it so fast if it was going to be difficult."

"He speaks!" I say.

"Are you going to share the timeline with me?"

"Five years."

"The operating profit you show five years out is almost three times our current performance. That ought to please our shareholders. James, tell me how you plan to deliver this level of growth."

"$0.5 billion in organic growth and $1 billion in acquisitions," I say. "We will have to achieve financial synergies over and above what we are able to achieve today from both the core business and the acquisitions."

"How will we pay for this, both the organic growth and the acquisitions, that is?" John asks, not in a judgmental way or a doubting way, but very coolly and matter of fact.

"Now, John, you have to realize that I couldn't even have drawn out those napkins yesterday, so please take my answers with a pinch of salt. I'm not trying to understate the level of difficulty here!"

John simply nods.

"My current thinking is that we will fund the organic growth through cash flow and we will have to do this without decreasing the dividends we pay to our shareholders; we are going to need everyone on board with us."

"The funds for the acquisitions will come from a mix of all the usual places, stock, leveraging the cash flow, and assets of the acquired businesses, debt offerings, and the banks. We will have to work it all out together, you, me and the other senior guys."

"What does the board think, are they driving you toward this?"

"No, no one is driving me. It's all internal so far, and you're the only one I've talked to. We have to hold this close to our vest and make sure anyone else we involve at this point does the same."

"James, you know I love you, but maybe you've just slipped over the edge. Please go home and allow someone to sedate you," John pauses.

"Now, what about Rory? Are you going to ask him to come in? We could certainly use his help on something as big as this."

"I'm not sure he's OK," I respond. "You know he almost broke down closing that business for us in Africa."

John just shrugs, "Who's calling him, James, you or me?"

"You call him, John."

We both get up and head for the garage, "I've got to get home, Martha expects me to take her and the kids to Suzie's dance recital. Believe it or not, hip hop is a real art form. What are you up to this weekend?"

"Pretty much the same as you, other than it's Jamie's soccer. I'll try to keep my head off this until Monday."

"Give me the documents," I say, taking the napkins and stuffing them into my pocket. "See you Monday."

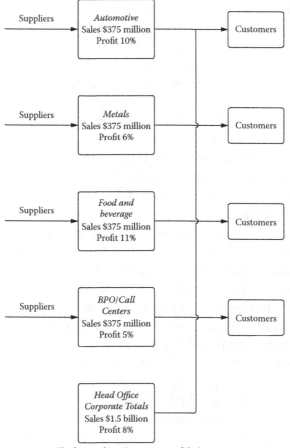

The first napkin: Current state of the business.

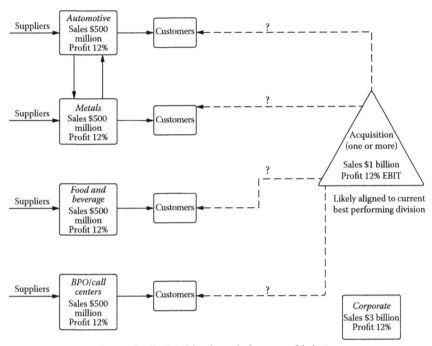

The second napkin: Initial thoughts on the future state of the business.

2

M&A in the Full Light of Day

Monday always seems to come around quicker than you would wish, and here it is. I'm at the office before 8:00; I always seem to do that, not so that others will think they have to, or even try to beat me in. I do it because I still have something to prove to myself every day and I want it to be obvious to everyone, purely and simply that I care.

Five minutes after I arrive, John walks into my office with two coffees. What a guy.

"I've been thinking about our discussion on Saturday," he says, "and I have a few very obvious thoughts before we begin boiling stuff down. Can I start?"

"What would you do if I said no?"

"Well, I'd know you were lying, playing me, having a bit of a laugh, and so I'd wait for you to smarten up."

I don't respond, so off John goes.

"Your plan has no margin for error; this thing will make us or kill us and so there are a few key elements that we have to think through right away. Things like when do we approach the chairman of the board, what detail does the plan have to be in before we do that, what impact will there be on the shareholders and when, how do we ensure we get the right person to help us find the right acquisition, how do we manage performance and grow the existing business during all of this, and finally do we need help from some sharp outsider to help with due diligence and integration?"

"Rory, for instance?" I ask.

John stops to draw breath, I was afraid he might never stop talking.

"Yes, well I'll need your help in answering every one of those questions before we go one inch further, John, and we ought to get the CFO in, don't you think?"

With no more ado I walk out of the office and go down the hall two doors, and there's Bill working away behind mountains of paper. Bill is old school, hell we all pretty much are.

"You got a moment, Bill?"

"For you, I have," and he picks up his coffee and follows me down the hall. When he spots John, he lets out a small groan. "What have I let myself in for?" he mutters.

"And good morning to you too, Bill," says John. "How was your weekend?"

"Good," says Bill shaking John's proffered hand. "I worked on sanding and varnishing one of my mates sail boat; a few of us are crewing with him this year."

"Sounds like fun," says John, sniffing his hand and smelling paint stripper.

"And what did you two guys get up to? I can't make out if you're happy or sad."

"I think what you are seeing is the in-between look, maybe more troubled than either happy or sad," I say.

"So what happened?"

John explained that I had an epiphany, a brain wave that could cause us no end of trouble or no end of joy, all still speculative though. He then gets up and walks over to my desk, flattens out the two napkins, and hands them to Bill.

After a few moments, Bill looks up with an accusatory look and showing no respect at all asks the question, "I see this blueprint for success is written on two napkins, were you drinking together at the time of their creation?"

John mocks indignation, "Yes, coffee." I don't respond at all.

Bill looks directly at me, "Who or what triggered this?"

"I did, buddy, all on my own-some lonesome. John was just unlucky enough to walk in and catch me looking out the window."

"That damned window," said Bill. "Who else has seen this?"

"Just us, Bill, we can still back out and keep face," I say. "But I think the three of us should bounce it around a little first." Bill nods his agreement.

Diane is outside my door at her desk, so I call her in and ask her if she can postpone the three of our commitments for the morning. She smiles, nods, and leaves, closing the door behind her.

I have a flip chart in my office, a throw over from my consulting days, and I walk over to it and pick up a marker. I explain that what's triggered me is that we are a rather large diversified business that crosses over between the manufacturing and service sectors, and although $1.5 billion a year in sales is not small, the fact that our focus is split between four diverse businesses makes us vulnerable to a takeover from larger more single product focused competitors. I state the obvious that in our current business environment, there are companies spending more than $3 billion on one acquisition, a lot more!

"When John came into my office this morning, he already had about six standout points that needed addressing, and I think the first thing we should do is focus on capturing those and then spend the rest of the morning adding to them, fleshing them out, and taking a shot at answering any questions they pose. If it all seems premature or overly dangerous, we can drop the whole thing, destroy the evidence, and get on with running this business as best we can, just like we did all day Friday and the day before, and the day before that too. We will have lost nothing more than half a day. If on the other hand we think that we have something here, we can set up the next steps, still just the three of us."

Bill asks the question that's top of mind, "How committed to doing this are you, James?"

"Not at all buddy; I want to do what's right for the business and I respect you both to the point of needing to hear how you think and feel about it. I'll drop the whole thing in a heartbeat if my thinking is wrong on this."

"Are you ready to get writing, James?" asks John, and he begins to call out his list.

- When do we approach the chairman of the board?
- What detail does the plan have to be in before we do?
- What impact will there be on the shareholders and when?
- How do we get the right person to help us find the right acquisition?
- How do we manage and grow the existing business during the five-year period?
- Do we need help from an outsider to help with due diligence and integration?"

We spend the rest of the morning fleshing everything out and decide to get back together Tuesday morning to determine if we are going to take this any further.

3

Preparing the Message for the Board

"Good morning, gentlemen." It's Tuesday morning and the boys have just arrived back in my office. Already this exercise is taking large chunks of our time, and we are just beginning.

"I'm concerned about the visibility of us sitting in your office first thing every morning like this," Bill says. "I mean, we can explain it away so far, but we have to change the venue from time to time or we will be causing concern among the troops."

"I'm sure we all agree with that one," John pitches in. "Why don't we just mix it up going forward and keep things low key for now."

"We need to involve Linda, our VP of sales, really soon," says Bill. "This level of growth will need her input. We had better get her into our next meeting."

Both John and I nod our agreement.

"OK, let's go over where we finished yesterday and add any other thoughts as we go."

I start; at the end of the day, this is going to be my baby. "I have to approach the board of directors through the chairman as soon as possible. A one on one with Alex in an informal setting should allow us to drop the whole thing and move on if it seems it's not going to fly; this could save a lot of unnecessary embarrassment and potential panic at all levels, all the way from the board to the shareholders, not to mention our customers and employees." The lads nod their agreement.

"I think we stay on message," says John, "that our business has to grow or potentially be acquired by a competitor or some private equity guys and potentially be broken up due to the diverse nature of our divisions. A $1.5 billion conglomerate that is publicly traded is not seen as a big business these days. Industry has come a long way since J.P. Morgan pulled

Carnegie steel together early in the last century to form U.S. Steel as America's first billion-dollar company. The merger and acquisition activity globally is hotter than hell right now with many of the single-company acquisitions ranging in price from $6 billion to $50 billion and higher, and so when it comes to a mid-size company like ours, it looks like it's grow or die!"

"We have to tell the chairman what this is going to mean from a financial perspective," adds Bill. "That we intend to double the size of the business over the next five years without saddling it with excessive debt. And that we will do this through organic growth to about $2 billion and acquisitions to the tune of an additional $1.0 billion in sales."

I'm happy with the way the guys are dealing with this and I weigh in with them, "I'll explain to Alex that we will keep this between a small team until we have drawn the first high-level project plan with all its implications to our stakeholders. That we will consider merging some of our existing divisions where appropriate to gain efficiencies and that we will minimize the cost of the organic growth of the business from $1.5 billion to achieve the targeted $2.0 billion while improving the overall profitability of the business in the process."

"When it comes to any acquisitions, it is likely that we will pay at least one times sales for the acquired company or companies, so it will likely cost us at least $1.0 billion. We should hone our acquisition and integration skills by doing a couple of small ones first, we can't afford to take risks with the high failure rate of acquired businesses, the statistics show that approximately 95% never attain the targeted synergy targets and financial expectations."

"We'll have to tell him how we are going to pay for all of this," says Bill, ever the guardian of the company's assets.

"Yes, we all know that the financials never work out exactly to plan, so there will have to be many contingency plans, but I'll take an initial stab at it. The organic growth will come from existing cash flow and the acquisitions will come from approximately 40% company stock, 15% corporate cash reserves, 20% in new bank debt, and 25% cash flow from the newly acquired companies. We have to do all of this without diluting the shareholders' dividends, and as long as we sequence and achieve the organic growth and increased profitability, we will be able to increase our share value for the final acquisition."

"It's just numbers," says Bill, "but it's a good start."

"These are big targets to achieve over a five-year period and if it was as easy as just saying it, then everyone would be doing it," says John.

"Yes," I say. "We'll have to assure Alex that we understand that this will require a complete business strategy to be developed to cover the coming five years, in which he and the board will be heavily involved at each stage of the development, and also in vetting the right person who will assist us in the search for the acquisition."

"And that my friend," says John, "is just the beginning. The ball is usually dropped during the due diligence process and the subsequent business integration. And then there is the question of resources, our current management will be pretty busy achieving the 33% growth required from our existing business and would likely be stretched to breaking point if they also had to integrate and manage the acquisitions, we'll need some help."

"Do you know anyone who fits the bill?," asks Bill.

"I do," says John, "and James knows him too!"

"Yes I do," I say, with a flash of foreboding.

"We've worked with him over the years, how many times has he let us down so far?" asks John.

"I hate to admit it, but the answer is never," my words come out as an almost croak.

Bill pipes up, "What's going on here? You two sound as though you're talking about the ghost of Christmas past!"

John answers the question, "There's a guy we've worked with off and on for more than twenty years; his name is Rory McGregor; he's an operations generalist and he's done almost every type of work for us. He never fails! He's sort of half executive and half consultant and he's run lots of businesses right up to the COO level, global businesses at that. He's also turned around a whole bunch of others working as a change agent."

"He sounds brilliant to me," says Bill, and when he meets with silence, he asks, "What's the problem?"

I answer, "Well, he's unorthodox and he's used to being his own man. You'll have to meet him."

"I'm looking forward to that," says Bill.

"You know he's been telling the world he's retired," says John. "And he's refused the last couple of assignments we've offered him. He can pick and choose, just doesn't need the money. Do you think he'll do it, James?"

"Oh he'll do it; it'll excite the hell out of him!"

"OK, I think I'm ready," I say. "I'll invite Alex to dinner tomorrow night and run all of this past him. I'll assure him that even with a go signal, we will set up the entire process as a series of go/no-go gates that we open and close one at a time over the five-year period and that each gate will act as a failsafe, ensuring we have to hit a predetermined success level before we move on to the next."

4

Expectations Are Reset on M&A Valuations

It's been an emotional day; people have been glued to the news networks, and no wonder! The geopolitical situation across the globe seems to be completely unstable, as far back as the fall of the Berlin wall and its impact on the relative strength of Russia as a world power to the reforms in China and the effect this has had in opening up of the world economy. It seems that there are bright lights on the horizon for improved standards of living for the world's people and that there is recognition that the continued growth and advancement of the planet will be furthered by having a healthy global economy that can feed and clothe the people. And yet each time we take a step forward, there is the constant threat of a step back: an oil tanker has a massive spill polluting the ocean, a train derails and explodes savaging an entire community, insurgents destabilize and terrorize entire countries, other countries militarize and threaten the whole world, famine and disease ravage continents, which, coupled with the inadequate distribution of humanitarian aid, cause misery and death to millions. Once stable conditions in the stock market like $100 for a barrel of oil change almost overnight to $50 and below, it's feast or famine in the global community and it is mirrored in the global financial markets. There is little stability in the world.

What does that mean to our company? We want to produce goods and services that the global community needs and wants, and, as much as our relatively small company can, support the continued redistribution of wealth as far and wide as possible. And yet we are a for-profit organization and so, of course, a portion of the earnings that remain after all costs will be shared among the shareholders of our company; after all it's the shareholders that make the rest possible. What remains is a small amount when you compare it to the total monies invested in the business. In fact, the average returns on equity for most firms are little better than what the investors could get by putting their money in the bank, and it MIGHT be safer there. It's a fact of life that some companies and their investors can experience substantial losses. It's no wonder the average investor will be very careful where they put their money!

There is no question that the distribution of wealth across the planet needs to be a lot better than it is today and I guess my viewpoint as CEO of this business conglomerate includes doing my part in helping with this while ensuring the well-being of our shareholders. I'm just a man, I enjoy my job, and it gives me a good living. I've chosen this as my profession a long time ago and I've worked my way through the ranks to arrive at these dizzy heights, and I don't take any of it for granted. I try every day to make the best decisions I can and to take the best actions I can to perpetuate the success of the business I am responsible for, and if I get this right, we will create more jobs and help improve the lifestyle of more families. Also, as we make diverse products across our divisions, we will produce among other things food, medicines, and useful services that can be made more readily available to the consumers wherever they are needed.

It might seem that a humanitarian viewpoint is at odds with a business viewpoint, but it is not to me. To me, business is personal and that does not make me so different from most of the business executives I know!

So here I am sitting opposite Alex, our chairman of the board. He is a good man and over the years, I have come to admire his judgment and integrity. We're sitting in a private backroom in Beppi's, Alex's favorite Italian restaurant, and both of us have just had the spaghetti Bolognese and the house's excellent meatballs—a very simple and delightful meal. The reason for the luxury of the private backroom is not for status but for privacy.

I've just gone over our thoughts so far on the company's growth during the coming five years and I'm glad Alex had the opportunity to digest his dinner before I began, as information as the second course seems to have given him indigestion.

"James, this is very bold and more than a little bit dangerous. Why now? The business is stable and the shareholders are happy."

"I believe it's time, Alex, I think it's grow or die! I hate being so dramatic and I get no pleasure in bringing ideas to you that carry this degree of risk, and yet here we are."

"So what do you want from me?"

"A couple of things. First, I want to hear your thoughts on the overall direction of the plan so far; I greatly respect your thoughts and opinion. Next, I would hope that you might be open to us creating a high-level strategy and project plan with all the positive and potentially negative implications of going forward. Unless, that is, of course, you decide to veto the idea, in which case we stop now."

"You know, James, you are very kind to give me your respect, and believe me that respect is mutual. What you do for the company is a factor in why at my age I continue to chair the board of directors, so, quite frankly, I can't ignore anything you say. And now that's out of the way, you can't put the genie back in the bottle!"

"The reason for the private meeting, Alex is intended to allow for that exact possibility—to be able at this early stage to squeeze the genie back into the bottle and cork it. This idea first saw the light of day less than a week ago and since then I've shared and received input on it from only two other people, both of whom you know well, John and Bill. There's nothing in writing at this point; you can indeed pull the plug without any fanfare."

"I understand that and I appreciate your tact, but it's not secrecy that makes it impossible for me to ignore this; it is the very real possibility that you could be right and to ignore it could be the wrong thing for the shareholders, so here we are."

"As you know, the board of directors meets once a month and the next meeting is in two weeks' time. Although you are the management representative on the board, I would ask you to absent yourself from that meeting."

My thoughts run riot; that one gives me a cold shiver. Have I gone too far? Whatever! What's the price of integrity?

"Don't worry, James," Alex says with a smile, picking up on my change in color. "I'd like you to do two things in the interim. First, write me a one pager capturing all that you have shared with me tonight and courier it to my office as soon as possible."

I nod my agreement.

"Second, start working on the high-level strategy and project plan, just you, John, and Bill, and any other senior executives you feel are absolutely necessary. I know that to ensure these are practical working documents, we will have to roll in the key stakeholders and subject matter experts at all levels, but for now let's keep it at the executive level."

I nod my agreement again. At this stage, I don't have a speaking part!

"I'll study your one pager and present its contents as a first blush to the board at the next meeting; I will of course not hand out the paper. If they feel it has merit, we will take it to the next step and I'll ask you, with John's and Bill's support, to present the plan at a special meeting of the board, which we will schedule for two weeks later, so you have four weeks to develop the plan."

"It's likely I'm going to support you in this, James, but if we go ahead and it fails, it may cost both of us our jobs."

"And I have one additional serious caution for you!"

"What is that, Alex?"

"If you end up targeting publicly traded companies for acquisition, you should expect them to be between 25% and 45% above book value! There are more buyers than sellers out there and that always drives the price up, so your expectation of buying a business that is $1 billion in sales for one times sales is unlikely. Although the price to earnings ratio of the major North American stock markets varies greatly over time, they are currently around 19 times forward earnings. When you add 45% premium to that, it will likely take most companies out of your reach!"

I pale, "So where does that leave us, Alex? Are we done before we start?"

"No...but you should likely target privately held smaller companies, possibly more than one. Private companies have no stock price, so no P/E ratio to consider, and also more often than not, smaller companies are less expensive than larger ones, size does matter!" responds Alex.

I thank Alex and we shake hands; he has given me a lot to think about. I pay the very modest bill, and we leave.

5

Getting Your Own House in Order...The Division President's Performance Update

This whole thing is becoming overpowering. I'm dreaming about it, but in reality, I suppose that's perfectly normal. When an important subject fills your conscious waking time, it will seep into your unconscious sleeping time, so I'm thinking my head off!

It's Friday morning, still week one since we started this grand adventure and it feels like we are just getting off the blocks. Strangely, at the same time it feels like it's been going on forever.

It's 8:00 a.m. and I'm sitting in the conference room with John on one side of me and Bill on the other. We are not discussing the impending five-year plan; that's on the docket for tonight after dinner. This morning the room is filled with the senior executives of our various operating divisions, everything from food to automotive, from metals to call centers. Those who could not attend in person have called in and are congregated through the speakerphone.

We go over the last quarter's numbers for each business division from sales through to profit, each leader taking the stage in turn supported by his finance guy and the rest of his senior staff. All of the numbers were sent in to John, Bill, and I in advance, so there is little in the way of surprise.

Following the financial report, we go over current and future hot issues and there are a lot of them! There are plenty of new threats and the same nagging old ones that don't seem to go away. It's sad but true to realize that we have been firefighting to keep this business on an even keel for years. On the surface, the combined overall company performance looks good, but when we peek under the bandage, there are some ugly sores that just don't seem to be healing. We hope to grow the sales of the business organically by 33% with a 50% growth in profits, and if we can't improve the existing business, we have no place in trying to finance and support major acquisitions.

I see the same frustration in John and Bill, both in their expressions and in their questioning of the division leaders; none of the three of us are viewing things quite the same as we did as recently as Monday. The culture change we will need to take us forward toward the achievement of our new goals will have to be handled very carefully.

It proves to be an exhausting day that grinds on until five in the evening and yet it seems really important to dine with the leaders of the divisions. John, Bill, and I will discuss the potential for the go forward on the M&A activity as time permits.

We have an hour after the close of the divisional update and the three of us sit in John's office to decompress. John is falling over himself with apologies for the operating problems inside the business.

"I'm sorry about this, James. I feel as though I've let things go for too long. On a day-to-day basis, I deal with all of the issues that come up, but sometimes, it feels like we are playing whack a mole—when we knock one problem down the next one just pops up."

"It's not just you buddy," I say. "We're all stretched; there are problems in sales and client services as well."

"Yeah," says Bill, "not to mention finance and admin; nothing ever runs as smooth as a top."

"It's going to have to…it's going to have to run a lot better than it does now," I fret, staring at the table.

All of us are silent, until I break it, "Let's take this hour to brainstorm the biggest issues we see in front of us right now," and we give ourselves a shake and get to it. The list looks like this.

- The acquisition we made two years ago in the outsourced call center space is floundering.
- Our operations in Quebec are losing money; they may need to be closed.
- We need to do a due diligence in Europe for a potential carve-out.
- Our automotive business is plagued by high costs and recurring problems.
- We have major inventory problems in the metals business.

"We have to stop here, guys. How bad can we be?" I get no answer, not a peep. "Well, if we resolve this lot, we will all feel a bit better, right?" There are no happy smiles, but there are nods of agreement.

"What about our mutual friend, John. Can he help us with this?"

John looks me straight in the eye; he looks slightly wounded, but he's a bigger man than that.

"Yes he can, James."

"Rory again," says Bill, "are you going to tell me about him now?"

John speaks up, "Sure...Rory McGregor has worked with both James and me off and on over the past 20 years. He's a good all-rounder and he gets the results."

"So what's the issue with him?"

I pick up the dialogue, "It might be fair to say he's a bit difficult to deal with, he has managed P&Ls across the globe, as well as having turned around businesses in various fields acting as a consultant. He thinks he's always right."

"It sounds as though he is," says Bill.

"That may be," John picks up, "but that doesn't guarantee it will be a ball of fun to work with him."

"I think he's mellowed over the years," I say, "but not without losing his drive, and so though he may cover it up, his aggressive nature lies just under the surface. I've seen him rip into his seniors when he feels pushed or even disrespected, and yet most people seem to love him. He treats everyone equally, but expects as much from them as he does from himself, and that's a lot."

"I think we should talk to him," says Bill.

"You still think he will do it, James?" asks John.

"If it interests him enough he will. I think he might be getting tired of retirement. We talked about this John, so call him and ask him in."

The rest of the evening goes well. It's always nice to spend time with the division leaders, and it's relaxing over a steak at the Scott House, but by the time the dinner is done it's 9:00 p.m., and I'm done, so we put off going over the meeting with Alex until Monday. Am I avoiding this?

6

Summary Update for the Chairman of the Board

It's Friday morning and we are producing the one-page document for Alex, including the strategic logic.

STRATEGIC LOGIC

At $1.5 billion in annual sales and as a diversified conglomerate, we are a ripe target to be acquired and potentially broken up. We believe there is more potential for unlocking shareholder value through making acquisitions and building from our business's current success.

Our intent is to grow the business to $3 billion over the coming five-year period—$0.5 billion to come from organic growth and $1 billion from acquisition. The intent is to work with the board of directors on a formal strategy to determine the prime product areas of the business, which we will target for growth through acquisition and organically; those we will maintain and support at current size; and any that we deem should be wound down.

As our current business interests focus on North America wide we will give high levels of attention to potential market share and geopolitical issues when considering any geographical expansion regarding potential acquisitions.

It is expected that the acquisition or acquisitions could cost us one times sales or $1 billion. To work within this pricing, we will target privately held smaller businesses. The funding of any acquisition is expected to come from company stock (approx. 45%), corporate cash reserves (approx. 10%), bank debt (approx. 20%), and cash flow from the acquired company (approx. 25%). It is imperative that shareholder dividends are maintained over the strategic time frame.

When the strategic objectives are aligned, we will appoint a single project leader who will monitor the correlated activities across all of our business interests.

As an often quoted statistic of acquisitions that fail to achieve all of the targeted financial synergies is 95%, it will be critical to ensure any target acquisition is a cultural fit with our business and that the due diligence and integration are executed flawlessly. To this end, we will ensure the broker we hire and the individual assigned to us is of the highest reputation and quality. We will also engage an experienced and respected expert to head up the due diligence and integration process. As our current executive team is expected to manage the organic growth of our core business, we expect the integration manager to manage the newly acquired business for at least the first twelve months.

The phases and dependencies for forward progress over the coming five years are (1) high-level strategic approach presented to the board, (2) contingent to board approval, the development of a five-year business strategy, (3) gradual involvement of a core group for planning and execution, (4) develop a project plan to cover the five-year strategic time frame, (5) conduct a confidential search for the right acquisition broker and begin the search for acquisitions, (6) trigger an in-depth business improvement process in our existing business to optimize profitability and grow the top line, (7) narrow down the target list of acquisitions and conduct site visits, (8) conduct necessary in-depth due diligence, (9) identify and quantify synergies, and (10) integrate acquisition or acquisitions.

Each Phase of the plan will be contingent on the successful completion of the previous phase. In this way, we will ensure a series of "gates" that must be closed during the overall journey to minimize risk.

Bill, John, and I review the two-page document and agree to courier it off to Alex, and when it is done, we sit together and catch our breath.

"Have you talked to Rory yet?" I ask John.

"I haven't been able to reach him. There's no special out of the office message on his phone, so I'm afraid I have no idea where he is. Sorry, James, it's my intention to keep trying."

"Well, by all accounts he's retired, so we can forgive him for not keeping office hours. I'll call him."

I walk back to my office and call Rory's cell phone. It's anonymous, simply telling me I've reached the number I dialed and telling me to leave a message, so I do.

"Hi, Rory, it's James. How are you, brother? Long time no talk. I need your help; can you give me a call? Be well, buddy."

I hang up, and within sixty seconds my phone rings, "Rory?" I ask, only half believing it.

"How are you, James?" answers the most familiar voice in the world.

"I'm great, buddy," I say, feeling immediately lighter. "It's great to hear your voice; it always makes me smile! How are you? Where are you?"

"Morocco. What's going on with you, buddy? Are you OK?"

"Yeah I'm fine! Are you working over there?"

"No, I'm on vacation, old friend, traveling Spain, Portugal, and Morocco with a beautiful woman."

I feel crestfallen; he's not going to be available. "I wanted to offer you a project, buddy."

"When do you need me in?"

"You haven't even asked what it is! When can you make it?"

"It'll take me two days to get out of here. Should I call you when I land and come round the office?"

"I don't want to ruin your holiday!" I say truthfully, but with my fingers crossed.

"It's all right, buddy; you sound as though you're in a hurry. See you soon."

And there's a click on the other end of the line; this shouldn't even surprise me. Truth to tell though he always amazes me!

I wander back down the corridor to see John and Bill.

"Did you get him?" says John.

"I did, he's in Morocco."

"So now what?" asks Bill.

"Oh he's coming, says he'll give us a call in about two days when he lands."

John doesn't look surprised, Bill is aghast! "Oh, hi, James," he mimics, "what's that? You need me? OK, mate, I'll be right there. Just have to organize a quick flight out of Morocco; see you in a couple of days."

"Just like that?" asks Bill.

"Just like that," says John, looking up for the first time. "It's a band-of-brothers thing."

7

The Help Arrives

"James? It's me, Rory. Good morning to you."

"Rory…how are you, buddy?"

"I'm good, pal. How are you?"

"I'm all right. Where are you?"

"I'm in your driveway, buddy."

I look out my bedroom window and there he is! How long has it been I wonder, six years maybe, and there he sits in an open convertible smiling up at me? I look at my wife and she has the broadest grin on her face. "I'll go get him," I say, clambering down the stairs.

I open the front door and we hug then shake hands, always an emotional moment.

"I've missed you, Rory."

"Yep, me too; sometimes we let things go for too long."

"That accent of yours always makes me smile," I say.

"I have an accent? In Scotland, they think I sound like an American! Where's your better half?"

And there's Martha with tears in her eyes hugging Rory's neck.

"Don't you ever stay away this long again! You know he pines for you, don't you?"

"I'm sorry, sweetie, I promise I won't."

"Where's Betsy?"

"We got an early check in, so she's settling into the hotel."

"Call her and get her over here!" says Martha…and it is done! Soon we are all sitting round the breakfast table as if no one had ever left. Betsy is the center of attraction.

"How was Morocco?" asks Martha.

"It was great," says Betsy. "The medina in Fez is over a thousand years old, and the square in Marrakesh is a cultural explosion, everything from snake charmers to belly dancers. Some guy just walked up to Rory and sold him two curved daggers. You know what he is like when it comes to collecting, so he couldn't say no. He almost threw them away, because he was worried about getting them through customs!"

"I'm sorry we broke up your holiday," says Martha. "Let's you and I go into the living room and you can tell me about everything that's been going on. You were in Spain and Portugal this trip as well I think?"

And off go the girls, leaving Rory and me together.

I sit with Rory and shoot the breeze until he asks me, "So what's it all about, James? Everything seems to be good in your life; it's not your health is it?"

"No, nothing like that; it's just work, buddy. And even that is no problem, more of an opportunity really."

"So, come on then, James, spill the beans."

"Oh for goodness sake, Rory, it's been six years since I saw you and you go straight to my issues...tell me what's been happening in your life!"

"Well I've been round the world a couple of times with Betsy, holidays though, river cruises, and all that stuff, but no work really."

"No work really, any work?"

"A little easy stuff, just a project here and there that interested me. I finally completed the much threatened book and it comes out in March of next year. It's a bunch of business and life experiences thinly disguised as a novel. Read it carefully, and you'll see yourself in it.

I've also got my French down to fluent, and learned enough about the financial markets to manage my own investments."

"What about your kids, all good I hope?"

"In general, yes, but with the usual ups and downs, no one keeps perfect health and no one's life runs exactly to plan...but all good in the scheme of things."

"What about you, James, what's been going on in your life?"

"A quiet life really, old friend. Martha and I are happy and the kids are great. Work has been a bit of a grind, and although it's still fun, it's not quite as exciting as it used to be."

"Why is that, James?"

"Do you remember you spun me a fable once about the difference between lighthouse keepers and lighthouse builders?"

"Of course I do, grasshopper; it's one of my favorites!"

"You told me there were two types of people in this world: lighthouse builders and lighthouse keepers. I think back in the day we both thought we were lighthouse builders, and it strikes me that you have been more true to yourself than I have…I think I've become a lighthouse keeper. It seems it's all been about keeping a steady hand on the tiller of the business, steady as you go with the occasional slight adjustment."

"And now, James? What about now?"

"I want to stand the business on its head and double it in five years through internal growth and acquisition!"

We both laugh, "Midlife crisis, James?"

"Shit no, Rory, I'm much too old for one of those!"

"So tell me about it."

I tell him everything that has transpired so far and why, and as would be normal at this point, Rory just listens. When I've laid it all out, I fall silent, and Rory maintains his silence too.

"So," I say, "speak!"

"What do you want me to do, James?"

"All of it. I need you to work with me and the team and make sure it happens."

"Project managers are ten a penny, James, not to take anything away from the role; it's a crucial one. But why me?"

"I don't want you to be project manager, Rory; I want you to be project lead. Your part in this will be as large…larger really than any other executive on the team. It will be far reaching, all the way out to every area of the business. You can of course keep your independent status as a consultant, if that's what you want, but I want you to act with the responsibility of a senior executive, with my authority."

Rory just nods his head, "OK."

"OK…is that it?" I say smiling. "I would like you to help me through the whole five years, pretty much full time."

"No problem."

He does this for me, but he'll never admit it! There's a big difference when I ask him if he would like a job or a project as opposed to when I tell him I need him. I've seen him fly half way round the world on three days' notice because I needed him to. It's more than friendship or good old-fashioned loyalty. We are truly like brothers, and this guy's net worth is in the millions!

"How do you want to start, James?"

"I think its two things, prioritize and sequence the change process, first their relative priorities and then any necessary sequence; they of course overlap and yet are two different things."

"Do you want to start now, buddy?" Rory asks.

Now it's my turn to nod and together we create the list:

- Finalize presentation for the board and get sign off.
- Formalize all milestones and gate activities for go/no go.
- Engage expanded executive team.
- Develop strategy for next five years and get sign off.
- Determine acquisition criteria.
- Engage acquisition specialist.
- Search out and narrow down acquisition targets.
- Site visits and due diligence.
- Integrate and achieve synergies.
- Manage new business to steady state.

Parallel to all of the above activities, we will perform the following activities:

- Set improved performance targets across current business.
- Achieve all improvement targets across existing business.
- Complete due diligence on European carve-out and determine go/no go.
- Integrate current acquisition (contact center business).

We survey the high-level list and determine who our project manager will be.

"We should get Smithy on this," says James. "He's the director of the project management team and he came from the ground up, so he is completely hands on and this helps with confidentiality and accountability."

"Rory, are you able to cover all four of the parallel streams of activities, working with handpicked teams of course, while still being part of the executive team working on the main acquisition stream?"

"I can. I'll be bouncing around a lot though and will have to tie into a lot of your meetings through videoconference, if that's OK."

"That'll work. I'll need you on site for the first two activities though, we have to complete the board presentation and then set the performance gates along the way. Kind of like compartmentalizing a ship's hull to avoid it sinking if one section gets breached. Doing this thoroughly will protect us from going too far if we find ourselves in a potentially bad situation. Also, I want you at the board presentation; they'll have to get a load of you sooner or later."

"We should get Smithy on board for all of this as soon as possible," Rory pipes in, "and we can do a first cut of the entire project plan, prioritizing and sequencing all of the major activities and resource requirements. This will allow us to do a backpass so that we can show the board that we can succeed in the time frame and within budget."

"Alright buddy, I'll get John, Billy, our CFO, and Smithy together in the boardroom for Monday at 10:00 a.m.; we'll continue until it's done. You ok with that?"

"Sure, it should be fun! Think about getting your top sales guy involved as soon as possible too."

"I intend to get her on board real soon, Rory. We want to grow the business as well as improve it, and I think you'll like her; she's a real pro."

For the rest of the day, we laugh a lot and talk about old times.

8

Establishing the Mandate and Gated Approach

I'm in the office by 7:00 Monday morning and so is everyone else—John, Bill, Smithy, and Linda, our VP of sales. I called John last night and he set it all up. All of the folks are keen to hear what is going on. I go through my meeting with Rory and all of the background info so far. The only ones surprised are Linda and Smithy; Linda is intrigued and it's obvious that Smithy is flattered to be included. Once again, we go over the need for absolute confidentiality and that it will be crucial to restrict the size of the circle and widen it on a strict, needs only basis.

We discuss next steps and adjourn our little impromptu premeeting until 10:00 a.m. in the boardroom.

John stays behind, "So, how's Rory?"

"He's great, at his best really, sharp and relaxed. I think being retired is good for him; it looks like Betsy is a calming influence."

"Is he going to be in for the duration?"

"Yes."

"Why? He got out in one piece and clearly he has his life set up so that he doesn't have to work anymore, so why is he doing it?"

"For the same reason you and I are still doing it, John, you know that."

"And remind me again why that is, James."

"Well, we both like to work, we like the challenge, the success and achievement helps, and we like to feel useful. And then of course, there is the ever unspoken, we do it for each other."

John just nods, "See you in the boardroom at 10:00."

And so here we are, Smithy has set up the boardroom with six stand-up flip charts and there are four laptops fired up on the table. Right on 10:00 Rory walks in, he hugs John, and they shake hands, both grinning from ear to ear.

"Long time no see, partner," says John. "You look fit and tanned, a little chubby maybe."

"Look who's talking," says Rory, poking John in the belly.

We are still a little formal at head office, so the four of us regulars are wearing collar and tie with Linda immaculate in a pin stripe pantsuit, Rory is traveling light from his trip to Morocco and so his concession to the hallowed halls and rarefied air is wearing a white cotton button down shirt with his jeans.

I introduce Rory to Bill, Smithy, and Linda, who have been watching our little homecoming with great interest. Rory gets quite formal with his handshake and greetings; he's pleasant, but he doesn't know these folks yet. They in their turn are analyzing his every move; I've told them a few war stories and they want to know if they are true.

"So let's get started," I say. "We are very informal about how we throw the stuff up against the wall in the development stage, so go right ahead, Rory. I've already told the guys that you are the project lead."

"OK, we have to start somewhere," says Rory, standing up and grabbing a handful of flip chart markers; he has never been the shy one!

"Let's make things visible so we can actually see each other's thoughts and make sure we don't lose any of them. Using lots of flip charts helps us keep the thread and sequence, and it lets us know where we have been and where we are going with our thinking. It also lets us see where there are holes in our plan and in our logic; we can fix any of those as we go along."

The team nod their agreement, because that's what we are—a team.

"We all know that this is a first rough cut, and that Smithy will fill in the blanks and produce the formal project plan," Rory nods to Smithy who acknowledges.

"So let's try this. We know it's a five-year plan to double the size of the company and so a working project statement might be

Over the coming five-year period, we will grow JKL Industries from a $1.5 billion corporation to a $3.0 billion corporation. This will be achieved by organic growth of $0.5 billion and acquisitions of $1.0 billion. We will improve our current EBIT from 8% to 12% in the expanded business. The business growth will be funded from cash flow, retained earnings within the corporation, company stock, and bank dept. The shareholders will be protected throughout the period and beyond with dividend continuity and a gated approach to ensure success milestones are achieved that limit risk before moving to each next step of the project.

Next, we sequence the steps we will take toward the acquisition and in parallel to them, we sequence the steps to achieve the targeted optimization and organic growth of the existing business.

Finalize board presentations	Set improvement targets cross business
Make board presentation/get sign off	Install improvement process/4-point plan
Develop five-year strategy	Achieve cross business improvement targets
Involve extended executive team	Complete due diligence on European carve-out
Engage acquisition specialist	Integrate current acquisition/achieve synergies
Investigate potential acquisitions	Ongoing cross business improvements
Conduct site visits/due diligence	Ongoing cross business improvements
Close acquisition deal	Ongoing cross business improvements
Conduct business integration	Ongoing cross business improvements
Achieve synergies	Ongoing cross business improvements
Manage "new" business to steady state	Ongoing cross business improvements

Gated approach to business improvement.

At the close of the five-year period, we will have achieved the following results from each of the two activity streams:

1. New business acquisition at $1.0 billion sales, 12% EBIT
2. Existing business at $2.0 billion sales, 12% EBIT"

"And there we have it, as easy as that!" Rory says with a smile "Any questions?"

Both John and I are silent, Smithy is writing at speed on his computer, Linda has a slight smile on her face but remains quiet, and Bill looks close to exploding.

"Do you really think it's that easy?" asks Bill.

I answer, "Do you see anything up there that is different from what has been talked about so far, Bill?"

"I guess not, James. It just all seems so black and white, and Rory writes it down and it's a done deal!"

Rory maintains his silence and John chips in, "I think one of the most valuable things Rory has brought to the table in all the years I've known him is his ability to take the mental leap and the courage to write it down in black and white. It's up to us to tear it to bits, amend it, scrap it, or commit to it. But there it is in front of us and, yes, it looks quite stark."

Rory speaks, "None of the above are my ideas; they are what I understand you have been talking about. James has asked me to help, and if I'm going to do that I need clarity, and I need to know the senior team is on board. If the opening project statement is wrong, then change it. If the sequences of the activities, or for that matter the activities themselves, are wrong, then change them. But speak now or forever hold your peace!"

"Explain your thinking a little please, Rory," I say, cooling things down a little.

"The boxes represent key activities that will lead us to the achievement of our five-year target, which in turn is represented by our project statement. Each box has two major activities, those to the left represent the path to our making a major acquisition, which will grow our sales by $1 billion per year and furnish a 12% EBIT. The activities to the right represent the path that will lead our current business from $1.5 to $2.0 billion per year, again yielding 12% EBIT. The right and left columns will run concurrently, and each box represents a gate, which can only be passed through the achievement of the quantitative financial targets ascribed to it and also the achievement of any qualitative targets we set.

The plan is of course incomplete and so will need refining and formalizing; if, however, we don't believe we can achieve the targeted results in the expected time frame when we look at them at this level, we have two choices. We either flesh them out now or quit. What do you say, James?"

"Guys, we are committed to the first box; we need to prepare a case for the board on the future of the business and we have to proceed toward getting our current business on track to achieve a 12% EBIT. I know that's a 50% profit improvement on a $1.5 billion business and I know that might seem more than a little scary, but I'm committed and I need you to be.

Rory will help us with this; believe me he is qualified to do so. He has my complete authority and will be treated the same as any senior executive in this business. When he speaks, you should consider I am speaking; that is how much faith I have in him. Working with John in operations, he will have complete authority and accountability for all of the items on the right-hand column. In addition to this, he will assist me every step of the way on the items on the left-hand column. Are you in?"

I think there is a lot of surprise around the table, but the nods seem to indicate everyone is in.

"What do you need me to do with this, Rory?" asks Smithy.

"Work with Bill and Linda, flesh out each major step with up to five substeps, consider resource requirements for each substep, and set it all up on a project plan. Consider any precedence relationships; take a first stab at the quantitative and qualitative measures to be met for progression from one gate to the next. Make it all fit inside a five-year time frame start to finish, and then do a backpass from the end forward to ensure it's not all a fantasy. Can you do that?"

"Yes."

"Can you get it back to James in the next five days?"

"Yes," repeats Smithy.

Rory smiles at me and comments, "I'm starting to like this guy already."

9

John and Rory Get Reacquainted

James has asked me to sit one-on-one with John; it's been a long time, five and a half years maybe.

I remember the first time I met John. He and James had been friends and had worked together forever. I was the new kid in town coming highly recommended to them as being the gold standard in problem solving. I taught them and eight of their senior managers a few techniques in rational process skills and they liked the results so much that they had me train the entire senior management cadre of the business they were running at that time. John was a great analytic thinker even then and so we found over time that we had a lot in common. I've always liked him; he is an honest and honorable man.

"How are you, Buddy?" I ask.

"I'm good, Rory. How are you mate?"

"Good, John. Look, I'm sorry to be here on your patch; I don't want you to think I'm pissing in your soup."

"Ah, Rory, my dear friend, you have the gift of the silver tongue! You're not pissing in my soup mate; I need the lift, and I need the help. Sometimes a man can get hypnotized by the swaying cobra. Existing long-standing problems can become the norm and fresh eyes can help."

"It's not everyone who sees things that way, John; they read help as some kind of threat."

"That's understandable I suppose, but not me, Rory, at least not where you are concerned, you're not the run-of-the-mill consultant."

"What am I then?"

"You're a known quantity, a friend, a fellow operator, and a decent bloke!"

"So will you be able to work with me?"

"Yes. Just remember that we're friends; be direct with me but respectful. If you show even an inadvertent sign of disrespect, my guys will begin to doubt me and lose faith."

"Have I ever been disrespectful to you before, John?" I ask, not as a challenge but as a health check on my own behavior.

"You never have mate, at least not deliberately! I know we're brothers." We both smile.

"So tell me about the business operations as if I know nothing, because in truth I don't know very much. Although I've helped on the occasional project here, the three musketeers have really never worked together in this company."

"JKL Industries, a conglomerate with $1.5 billion in sales and 8% EBIT, steady as clockwork. We pay the same 3% dividend to our shareholders year after year, and along with a steady 3% appreciation in our share price even in a downmarket, we are considered a value company."

"We have four divisions—automotive, metals distribution, food and beverage, and business process outsourcing (BPO), which is the baby of the group, a two-year-old acquisition. Strangely all four have leveled off at about 25% of our revenue, so approximately three hundred and seventy-five million in sales each."

"What about profitability?"

"Food is best at 11%, auto is next at 10%, metals is at 6%, and the BPO business is lagging at 5%."

"How do you feel about that, John?"

"Well, as you know very well, Rory, the numbers seldom come from exactly where we think they will. Running a P&L is a balancing act; you take the good guys when you can to help smooth out the bad guys. And the results tend to move around; it's like playing whack a mole. It's also a balancing act between repeat problems and one time issues and costs. The fact of the matter is that $1.5 billion at 8% EBIT is right on budget, and so until now I thought I was doing all right."

"And now?"

"And now I know I have to do better, a lot better."

"How do your division heads feel about their performance?"

"Just like you would imagine. Food and auto think they are doing great, and, in truth, we will have to get really creative to get food up to 12%. Metals say it's the point they are at in the business cycle, and BPO say they are being squeezed by new global competition. We never quite achieved the synergies we expected when we acquired this one two years ago."

I become very sensitive to John's feelings, "So how do you think we should tackle it buddy?"

"Well, we can't tell the division heads about the planned acquisition as yet, so I think we start with introducing stretch profitability targets of 2% points each for food and auto and tell metals and BPO that we need them to hit the 8% budgeted number that the company expects to achieve. We tell them we can't stand still or we'll be left behind. I tell them that I know we recognize it's not quite as easy as the snapping of fingers, but that you've made a life's work of this sort of thing and that you've helped me and James with profitability in the past and you are going to help them... and me, now!"

"I expect they are going to love that," I smile.

"Just like you and me, Rory, they have no choice, other than to leave, that is. When we achieve this preliminary target, we will be at an average EBIT of 10%, a good step toward the 12% we need."

I agree, "I like the idea of taking it in bite-sized chunks, there is no rule that tells us we can't keep right on going as new opportunities surface from our improvement work. And even when we get to 12% EBIT, we still have to grow the top line by 33%, maintaining the higher level of profitability."

"The sooner we can tell them about the intended overall company growth, the better," John says.

"Agreed, but that's not yet. One step at a time old buddy, are you going to bring the division presidents in?"

"I'll set it up for tomorrow afternoon, just you, me, and the four of them."

We meet in the boardroom at head office next day at 1 p.m. John handles the introductions, "Hello, everyone. Let me address the elephant in the room straight away." Everyone laughs and John continues, "Actually, he's not really an elephant; they don't have elephants in Scotland and this beastie is definitely Scottish. I'd like to introduce you to an old friend of mine, Rory McGregor. He and I have worked together a lot over the years, as indeed he has with James, in both cases in many guises."

There is interest in the room but also apprehension. Do they have a new boss, they wonder?

"Let me put any concerns you may have to rest straight away. Rory is not signing on with the company as a new executive and neither James nor I are going anywhere."

There is still a lot of tension and curiosity in the room; they know I have not appeared for no specific reason at all.

"Rory is a consultant and he is going to work with all of us to help optimize the business's performance."

The tension in the room has now risen considerably; I'm still silent as indeed are they.

"Although Rory will not be joining us as an executive, he will have executive authority, both James and mine, and it is expected that everyone will treat him as such."

Dead silence, and John is visibly a little uncomfortable.

"Please go ahead and introduce yourself, Rory."

"Hi, I'm Rory. I'm no spring chicken, so please be aware I'm not after anyone's job. John and James have brought me back from retirement to help the company grow past a few major targeted milestones and then it's back to my hammock in the sun."

There are a couple of smiles in the room and a couple of stony faces, just about par for the course really. These are senior executives and they don't need anyone to help them tie their shoe laces.

"I style myself as half consultant, half executive because that's the path life has taken me down, and so I'm neither fish nor fowl. I've turned around more than five businesses as a consultant and managed companies all over the world. In between, I've done all the Joe jobs you could imagine, from office boy to engineer to COO. My work has been in various industries: engineering, high-speed packaging, automotive, BPO, food, pharmaceutical and metals processing and distribution, and plastics."

"That's me," I wrap up.

"Thanks, Rory, for that enlightening introduction," John adds dryly. "Can we go round the table and introduce ourselves to our new colleague?"

It seems we always go clockwise with these things, and first to speak is a large burly man.

"I'm Dave Mason, president of our metals division. I've been with the company twenty-five years. I started by pushing a brush and did every other job between that and this. I'm proud of this company and my part in it and it grieves me a little that it is considered we need external help."

"Thanks, Dave," says John and he nods to the next in line.

"Good day. I'm Harry Wordsworth and I head up our automotive division, just like I've heard you are I'm a man of few words, and like Dave I've been here a long time. I started as a tool and die maker and worked my way up to these dizzy heights. JKL Industries has trained me in process tools like Six Sigma and nurtured me in allowing me to grow. I'm keen to see what you will bring to the party that we are not already doing."

"Thanks, Harry," and John nods again in the direction of the next lucky contestant.

"Hello, I'm Jennifer Allen, president of our BPO division. I've got twenty years BPO experience and have been with JKL Industries for two years, since the BPO division was acquired. It's nice to hear you have BPO experience and I look forward to the help."

"Thanks, Jennifer," says John, "You're even briefer than Wordsworth!"

There's a slight chuckle around the room. Good, we need the ice broken. John nods again.

"I'm Tony Dent and I head up the food division. I've been in the company for two years and was head hunted from one of the major industry leaders in our field. I like it here, good people and a great company."

"Thanks Tony," says John. "So now there is a burning question or two in the room I'm sure. Go ahead and ask, Rory, and I will answer."

"Why now and why him?" asks Dave.

"I'll pick that one up," says John glancing over at me. "We have to grow, both in top-line sales and in profitability. We have to grow a lot…33% in sales and 50% in profitability. Our performance has been flat for years and so we can benefit from a catalyst to get things moving; Rory is such a catalyst."

"33% in sales and 50% in profitability is a lot," says Jennifer. "Will it be a flat increase across the board in all four companies? And what is the timeline?"

"You take this one, Rory."

"Quite a lot to answer, Jennifer, and yes 33% and 50% is a lot, and yet that's the target we have been set by the CEO and so we have to get behind it. We will look at every division together to determine the degree of opportunity that we can see and then establish targets, so likely the expectation will not be even across all divisions. However, it means that there will be higher targets in some divisions to offset any lower goals in others. The overall company targets remain 33% and 50%. The time frame is five years, although there will be stepped targets during this period."

"Will you be here for the five years?" bursts out Tony.

"That's the plan," I answer.

"How will we achieve such huge performance improvements?" asks Harry.

"The usual stuff," I answer. "Some of it straightforward, some of it sheer brilliance, most of it common sense with some flashes of genius from all of us. That's if we work as a team, but none of it will be outside our capability."

They think I'm being flippant; I'm not!

"So what will you actually do?" asks Tony.

"Together with you four good folks and John, we will establish cross-functional teams to analyze each business and draw up a list of opportunities for improvement. We will then quantify the value of each target initiative, prioritize and sequence them, and achieve the targeted results. I will be front and center with all of this, as will each of you. My part is to play a major role in this team; I'm not the Lone Ranger."

"Wouldn't we have a better chance at this size of growth through acquisition?" asks Harry.

I glance at John and he answers, "Maybe, but our target is to achieve this growth organically. Let's get this part right and then we might start talking acquisitions."

Silence settles on the room as they digest the information; after all we haven't asked them for their recommendations on where we should hold this year's Christmas party!

"So what's next?" asks Dave.

"Rory will call you and set up site visits for early next week. In the meantime, I'd ask you to each identify four or five folks from your divisions to work exclusively on the improvement project, and I will interview them with Rory. Don't send us folks that just happen to be available. Send us hot shots, cross-functional hot shots; the future of our company depends on it."

John draws the meeting to a close, "Thanks for coming in, guys; I know you're busy. Oh, by the way, I'll be coming in with Rory for the site visits next week."

10

The Search for Our M&A Broker

"What do you think, Alex? What did the board think?"

It's the day after the board meeting and Alex has asked that I meet him here with my core team at head office. And so here we all are in the boardroom.

"I think the direction is right, and so does the board. Everyone is a bit skittish about it of course; this is the biggest expansion plan that any of us has ever been faced with before. You and your team have alleviated a great deal of our concern by your approach so far. We like it that you have thought out the steps in detail right up to the first go/no-go gate and that the plan beyond that has also received careful attention. So tentatively, it's a go. Let's see how we all feel about the progress and the second stage of the planning process when we reach the first gated milestone."

We all thank Alex for his support and belief in us; we show no hint whatsoever about the fact that we feel the pressure of the journey that is now set in front of us.

"Do you know anyone you could recommend as an acquisition broker?" I ask. "Realizing that we are probably a year away from finding the right project, and then proving it out by due diligence, we should engage the right broker now."

"Easier said than done of course," says Alex. "We need someone we can trust and who will give us the time and personal service we require. In fact, there's a whole list of important criteria in picking the right broker."

Rory is unobtrusive as he stands up in front of a flip chart and picks up a marker pen, but Alex appreciates the formality and respect that this implies.

Alex calls out the list.

- Exclusivity
- Same broker at all times

- Track record in our search area
- Paid only if he or she finds the company we acquire
- Prepared to present multiple detailed options
- Prepared to do site visits on the short-listed alternatives
- Broker does initial negotiations with prospect
- Broker deals with points of contention with both parties
- Has an acceptable fee structure
- Works well and is compatible with our team
- Has a first-class reputation and references

"This is only a start, but you get the drift," says Alex. "You and the team will add other criteria. When you are ready, we will interview possible candidates together and judge them against these objectives."

"So, not to be pushy, Alex, but do you have anyone in mind?"

"I have three possible candidates in mind, yes. Two of them are private individuals who have their own small firms and the other is a partner with one of the big houses. Each of them is well qualified technically to do the job for us, but they are of course all different. Even if we think the ideal candidate is within the group, we will still have to interview each to see which one fits best. At the end of the day, best fit covers a lot of ground."

"Who would you recommend conducts the interviews," I ask.

"This entire group should be part of the team, including myself of course. That way, if one or two of us can't make it for a specific interview, we will still have a quorum."

The meeting has largely been a two-way interaction between Alex and me, with Rory on the pen, but the entire group is still engaged and expresses their agreement.

"You will have to flesh out the criteria for the search prior to meeting any broker; he or she will ask questions, you know. As long as we trust the individual coming in and that they have signed a confidentiality agreement, we can answer high-level questions regarding the targets."

"Yes of course, Alex," I agree. "We have done some preliminary work on which sector or sectors of our business we should expand through acquisition, keeping in mind your thoughts and advice regarding the premium on book value usually paid for large public companies. We have also considered the favored geography; we will flesh it out and present it to you within the next two weeks and prior to any meetings with perspective brokers."

"Good," says Alex. "Now, you are approaching this business expansion on two major parallel fronts, where do you currently stand on the organic expansion and business optimization?"

John picks this one up, "Rory and I have already had a preliminary meeting with our four division presidents; we have made them aware of the initial improvement targets and their part in achieving them. Rory has made a follow-up phone call with each and set up individual meetings at their locations for next week; both of us will attend and set the groundwork for a business analysis in each division. It's our expectation that this will trigger us into the selection of four teams that will conduct the analysis under Rory's direction."

"Good," says Alex. "I expected no less of you. Do we have anything else for today, James?"

"Guys?" I ask the room, and there are no further questions. "When do we start the interviews with the brokers, Alex?"

"I'll give you a call, James," says Alex rising and shaking hands with the team.

"I'll walk you down to your car," I say.

"What did you really think of the meeting, Alex?"

"I'm encouraged; I like your team and your methodical approach."

Alex pauses at his car, "This one is really important James; I won't survive as chair and you likely won't as CEO if we botch it. Just make certain that strict confidentiality is held all the way through; in fact, have your team sign a confidentiality agreement on this. I trust them and yet I know there is something in signing your name to an important document that engenders the need to ensure its expectations are met as you expand your circle of those in the know. Sign it yourself so that your folks know they are not being singled out or distrusted. Other than that James, just make sure your short-, medium-, and long-term planning is sound, and focus like crazy on meeting or exceeding all the targets up to each gate."

"Thanks, Alex," I say, shaking his hand.

"Talk to you soon, James," Alex actually smiles.

11

Expect Resistance: Doing the Rounds with the Division Presidents

"Are you ready for this, Rory?" asks John. "This guy may take a bite out of your neck!"

We've just pulled up outside the head office of the metals division to meet with Dave Mason.

"Sure," I say.

John looks at me quizzically, "Is there nothing that fazes you?" he asks.

"Everything fazes me, John; I just try not to show it and I certainly can't afford to let it stop me."

"What do you really think of this guy anyway, buddy?" I ask.

"Well, he's as hard as nails, a bit of a bully maybe, and knows the metals business inside out. I don't think he'll be keen to have you tell him how to run things."

"I get that," I say, "but at the meetings we've had so far I got the impression it was your business not his! And it's as much your neck, and James's for that matter that's at stake here as mine. We signed up, John, and for me, there is no backing out. How about you?"

"Same mate," says John, slightly red in the face. Clearly, I didn't have to remind him we were all in this together, my bad.

The head office is stitched onto the front of a major plant location, a nice front desk for reception and a few offices for Dave, the plant manager, the controller, and the sales guys. There's a steady flow of traffic in and out of the plant, all normal so far.

The receptionist calls Dave and he comes out to meet us, "Good to see you, John," he says, shaking both of our hands. "This way, gentlemen," and he leads us to the conference room. A smiling guy in a spaghetti-sauce-spattered white shirt stands up to meet us.

"Hi, John," he says shaking hands and then offering me his handshake. "Hi, I'm Aldo, the division controller."

Dave laughs, which breaks the tension. "We all feel safe to start lunch once Aldo has had his first forkful of spaghetti."

Aldo looks down at his shirt disappointedly, then dabs at it with the tip of his handkerchief "Sorry, guys, I have no idea why that always happens."

We grab a coffee from the end table and sit down. Dave starts, "John, I know I have a bit of a reputation for being difficult and a bit of a know-it-all, but I want you to know that I'm completely committed to this initiative, I hope it's OK with you that I've asked Aldo in."

John seems a little surprised, but says that's fine and that he's glad Dave is committed.

Dave turns to me, "We don't know each other, Rory, but I'm certainly looking forward to getting to know you. I've Googled you and it seems you've been around the block. Also, John and James speak highly of you, and that, from my personal experience, is worth something. I'm not the easiest guy in the world to get along with, and on the face of it neither are you; I hope we can make our similarities work for us instead of against us."

"That would be good," I say, "It feels like we are off to a good start here."

It's John's turn to take the floor and he repeats the general mandate for Aldo's sake, "We have to grow across the entire company, $1.5 Billion to $2.0 in sales and 8% EBIT to 12%. I'd like to say let's not make a big fuss of it but that would be futile; it's a big deal and everyone across the company will end up involved. What I really need you to do though is control the rate of communication, if you go too fast, you will scare the troops and if you go too slow, they will think we are hiding something. Every closed door potentially says as much as every information meeting."

"So how do we get over that, John?" asks Dave.

"You know Helen Morris at head office? She is our public relations and communications officer and will be working with us to craft our communication strategy. We haven't engaged her yet; we are moving kind of fast and yet we are expanding the circle as slowly as possible on a need to know basis. Clearly, Helen needs to know, but we thought we would do the round of one-on-ones with the division presidents first. On retrospect, we might have got that wrong, so please assume a high level of confidentiality is required until she reaches out to you in a week or so."

Everyone nods their agreement.

"So how much do you need from metals guys?" Dave asks.

"Start with 10 percentage points on sales and 2 points on EBIT, that's less than we will eventually need but it's challenge enough to be getting on with," John replies.

Aldo scans the numbers in front of him location by location, looks up, and nods at Dave, who in turn nods to us.

"What can we get started on now?" asks Dave.

I kick in, "There are a few ways of finding opportunities, we should do the easy ones first, there will be time enough for any blood, sweat, and tears, although luckily we will not be having mass layoffs as we are in growth mode. What Aldo just did usually leads to the low hanging fruit. Compare the achieved financials with target, compare the locations to each other, compare product lines with each other, look at the inventory turns and compare them location to location, look at sales performance against plan, those sort of things."

"Next we should look at the known repetitive problems and fix them where we can."

Dave and Aldo are taking notes, this is good!

"We would also like you to identify four or five guys to help us with combing the business for additional opportunities. Don't go for who just happens to be available, rather go for hot shots, guys you trust and who you would like to grow. I'll teach them analysis skills and work with them throughout the process. Go for cross-functional where possible so that they can benefit from each other's experience and point of view."

"Do you want to meet them before they are made the offer?" asks Dave.

"Thank you for suggesting that, Dave; I think that's a great idea. You, John, and I should meet them for a panel discussion here in your board-room, the candidates one at a time with the three of us. If we get this right, these guys will also become our champions in implementing change."

"Anything else for now, guys?" John asks.

"No, it's all good," echo Dave and Aldo.

"Good meeting," says John. "Thanks for your commitment. I know it seems like a bit of a fuss, but I'll need you to sign these confidentiality agreements, all of us are signing them, James, me, Rory, and Bill, all of us. Courier those to me at head office when you have read and signed them."

And with that we leave.

"What do you think, Rory?"

"Good, a great start, I expected resistance."

"Me too, do you think everyone will be this easy?"

"Nope!"

In the next two days, we visit each of the remaining businesses and feel that we have made good progress for the week.

"So tell me Rory, what did you think of the week?" asks John.

"Good, we got everything done that we had to; doing too much in a short time frame is as bad as delaying getting started."

"Ah, the profound warblings of the Celtic tongue," says John, looking at me with as much patience as he can muster.

"You would like more, John?"

"Uh...yes."

"Well, Dave was pretty much what we would have wanted him to be, he has affirmed he is on board, but do not be surprised if we have to remind him of his commitment from time to time before this thing is done, and I like Aldo, he's clued in. The trick with Aldo is going to be finding him through the haze of spaghetti sauce during lunch time in the cafeteria."

"The other three were a mixed bunch. I think Tony Dent is afraid for his job, which is rather sad when you think of it; he's a smart lad and his business is performing reasonably well. I think it might be due to his being so new to the company and still feeling he has to prove himself."

"Well he does have to prove himself; all of us have to!" says John.

I move on.

"The lady who runs the BPO business is interesting. She seems to be completely on board and she sure is smart. I get a sneaking feeling though that she thinks the overall performance of her business is a bit out of her hands."

"She's not completely wrong in that now, is she, Rory?"

"True, she has minimal control over some of the things she faces, some driven by customers and some by global events and trends. However, both she and you and I for that matter have to assume that we can influence... everything, even if it's more true for some things than it is for others, the results will come from a mishmash of activities and we have to swing at every ball with confidence. I'm not concerned about her; she just needs our support and encouragement."

"And then there's the guy at automotive."

"Can't you even remember his name, Rory?" There's exasperation in John's voice and glance.

"Sorry, buddy, not always. I have so many things buzzing around my mind that occasionally I draw a blank. Let me think...Wordsworth!

Don't worry though; more often than not a combination of hard work and the grace of god brings back all the needed bits of information at the right time. Also there is the distinct possibility that I am actually having a very real senior moment. You know how old I am, don't you?"

None of this seems to placate John, so I continue.

"I think he's a good guy and I think he is a little traumatized by the extent of the task in front of him. I believe our job is bigger than asking for or demanding improvements; we really have to be there with them in the trenches finding and executing the opportunities. It'll all be fine; don't worry."

"You astound me with your unswerving confidence, Rory, you always have. How do you do that?"

"The truth is, John, that my life has never given me an option, I've always had a living to make, a family to feed, and a roof over our head to pay for. From my early days as a tool and die maker to the running of businesses, I was ever only as good as my last shift, my last results, my last performance. Why would anyone hire or pay me if I don't get the results? They simply wouldn't! So I've always had to get the results; it has formed a habit, and I use it to my advantage."

John nods, "It's turned you into a tough son of a bitch."

"Well gee…thanks, John," I do my best American accent.

I continue, "Early next week we will interview the teams who will help us conduct the businesses analysis, then I will train them, and we can move to the next stage."

"We have given them a target of an initial 10% growth in their existing business, we will achieve that and continue to achieve a further 10% year after year, and this will get us the 33% sales growth we need from the business in about four years or so, not bad."

"How do you see us achieving that?"

"Not sure yet buddy, but I have a few ideas, I'll tell you more definitively in a month or two when we have analyzed the business and got to know the folks a bit better."

"You make it sound so easy!"

"It's not easy! It's grim! But it's possible! It won't come from exactly where we think or exactly when we think it will, but we have gates to meet before progressing from step to step, so if for any reason we find it impossible to hit the overall target, we will still have a stronger business for the effort."

"Finally, we are asking for 1 percentage point improvement per year in EBIT for the whole business that will get us to 12% EBIT by the close of year four. Believe it or not buddy, if there is an easy bit that's it!"

"I'm glad you're helping us with this, Rory," John says, slightly subdued.

"Me too, John, and I'm glad to work alongside you; you're a good friend from way back. Don't worry mate, it'll be easy."

John shakes his head and we both laugh.

12

The Strategy Review

I have asked the core team to an off-site meeting at a local hotel. It's time we talked about strategy, and we have John, Bill, Linda, Smithy, and Rory in the room.

"Welcome, lady and gentlemen. I'm sorry to have taken up your full day with so little notice; I'm not sure how far we will get in eight hours or so but I think it's time to make a start. How often does anyone here look at our current strategy?"

"Not often," says Bill.

"Same here," says John. "Don't get me wrong James; I know what it is but it's been so long since we formulated it that it's turned into steady as we go!"

"I'm afraid that's true for me too," Says Linda.

"I look at it," I say, "but I have to say it has not driven my behavior of late; it's really not meant to be that way. What's the point in saying we will be the best in our industry if we are not striving for exactly that and then knowingly settling for less?"

"We have annual operating plans that support the budget," says John, "and they reflect the strategy."

"I understand guys, I really do, and it's my failure. It's the CEO's job to ensure the business is operating in line with its strategy and if for any reason, there is a disconnect to do something about it. It's pretty obvious that the expected growth in our business over the next five years is totally out of line with the current strategy and so we have to do something about it; this is an opportunity."

"Rory, would you facilitate this meeting for us?"

"Glad to," says Rory moving to the flip charts.

"I want this strategy to be a living document," says James, "something that we meet to review frequently so that we can determine if we are moving toward the desired state. It should also be something we are not afraid to challenge and add to or subtract from if we feel we must. It takes a lot of time and energy to develop a strategy and by god I do not want one that gathers dust on a shelf."

Clearly, everyone in the room agrees.

"How do we start, James? Shouldn't we have some of the other senior executives present?" asks Bill.

"We should and we will old pal, but not quite yet. I still think we have to control the size of the circle for a while longer. Once we have taken a first run at it and shown it to Alex, we'll include the others and round it out. I'm still nervous about the acquisition thing getting out."

"Should we get the main categories on the board first?" asks John.

- "We should," I say, calling them out, with Rory writing them down.

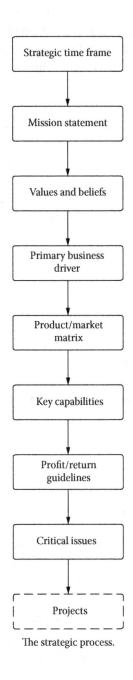

The strategic process.

"You've been thinking about this, James," says Rory.

"I have, and still I may have missed some major categories, but the trick here is to get started and to progress this thing with a minimum of bullshit and navel gazing. Our first cut at it will not be the last and against my better judgment, we will likely end up padding it a bit so that it will pass the weight test!"

"Shouldn't the critical issues lead to projects?" asks Smithy.

"They should and they will," I respond. "The critical issues are the bridge to the projects, and the projects will be a key element of our strategic follow-up, but they are in themselves not actually part of the strategy. Call me old fashioned."

We mess around with the sequence of the key elements a bit and add strategic time frame as the first element, and then together we brainstorm the content of each element step by step.

STRATEGIC TIME FRAME

The strategy will serve as our vision; it will guide us and drive the actions to be taken by JKL Industries over the coming five years. There will be biweekly strategic reviews to assess the achievement of our major goals and objectives and to weigh our major decisions against the companies stated intent. The strategy will be formally reviewed at least annually with the input of the board of directors to ensure its continued validity and relevance.

MISSION STATEMENT

JKL Industries will continuously strive to be one of the top three companies in each of its chosen business sectors, if not in size, in quality and reputation. It will operate businesses in metals processing and distribution, automotive, business process outsourcing, food and beverage processing, and sales. Any new products, services, or markets we enter will be in line with our core capabilities. Our primary geography for our products and services will expand from our North American base to encompass offshore locations and markets globally.

VALUES AND BELIEFS

- Ensure an above-average return to our shareholders.
- Truth and honesty with our employees, customers, shareholders, and suppliers.
- Respect for the planet and the communities within which we operate.
- Commitment to the well-being of our people.
- Produce only safe and healthy products and services.
- Open, honest, and approachable management.
- Share the success of our company with our people and the community at large.

PRIMARY BUSINESS DRIVER

The primary business driver of JKL Industries over the coming five years will be profit/return. We will consider expansion into any area of product and services that meets our key capabilities and our profit/return guidelines so long as it does not violate our values and beliefs.

KEY CAPABILITIES

Those that we have or would develop

- In-depth management and superior content capability in our chosen fields
- The ability to continuously improve our business performance
- A satisfying pay for performance culture
- A superior global sales presence
- Decentralized authority and accountability
- The ability to acquire and integrate acquisitions while achieving targeted synergies

PRODUCT MARKET MATRIX

Products →

Markets	Food and beverage	Pharma and vitamins	High end confectionery	Auto parts	Auto assemblies	Metals	BPO/marketing	Transport	Canned goods
Tier 1 autos	H→H Future/Grow/Current	H→L Future/Grow/Current	M→L Future/Grow/Current	H→H Future/Grow/Current	M→L Future/Grow/Current			H→M Future/Grow/Current	H→H Future/Grow/Current
Own stores	M→L Grow	M→O Explore	M→O Develop					H→L Grow	M→O Explore
Other stores								H→L Grow	
Big box	M→L Explore	L→O Explore	L→O Explore					H→M Grow	M→O Explore
Manufacturing				M→O Explore	M→O Explore	H→H Future/Grow/Current		H→M Grow	
Construction						H→M Grow		H→M Grow	
General auto						H→M Grow	H→M Future/Grow/Current	L→O Explore	
Financial services							H→M Grow		
Other							M→M Explore	L→O Explore	

Product/marketing matrix.

Profit/Return Guidelines

Each Division of JKL Industries is currently approximately 25% of the overall company sales. It is the intent that each division will also contribute 25% of the overall company profits. Available growth capital for organic growth or growth by acquisition will be allocated in proportion to the success of each division.

Overall company financial expectations expressed as a run rate in the last quarter of each year.

Year	Sales	Profit
One	$1,700,000,000	9% EBIT
Two	$1,800,000,000	10% EBIT
Three	$1,900,000,000	11% EBIT
Four	$2,000,000,000	12% EBIT
Five	$3,000,000,000	12% EBIT

Note: Year five results are contingent on the closing one or more major acquisitions from year two forward and in the fourth quarter of year four.

We've stopped for a bite of lunch, a sandwich and a can of pop and a chance to slow our racing minds for a few minutes.

"What do you think of the show so far, guys?" I ask.

"Terrifying," says John.

"Scary as all hell really," says Bill. "How can we expect to grow the business at up to 10% per year when the GDP for the United States is only growing at 2%? In fact that's pretty much true for the developed world, and even China is only growing at around 7%."

Smithy says nothing and Rory also remains quiet.

It's John's turn again, "I can't help but notice that we have gone from acquisition singular to acquisitions plural. I know you discussed this with Alex, but I'm not quite sure where your head is on it."

"It's all about the premiums that have to be paid over book value for large publicly traded companies, John, they can be as high as 45% over their current stock value. If we buy a $1 billion company, it could cost us almost $1.5 billion and that's the size of our current sales! I simply don't believe we can afford it."

"So does that mean we are done?" asks Bill.

"Not by a long shot, Bill," I reply, "But it means we have to get smart and figure out how to buy some smaller privately held companies that can yield real synergies with their addition to our current base business. I was hoping we could start working on it today after the strategy work. I have some ideas I hope we can build on as a team."

"Well, OK then," smiles Bill, "I'm enjoying this too much to be OK with it coming to a sudden end!"

"Now back to your earlier point on our ability to grow the business at 10% per year in the current global economy, we have to know what we are signing up for over the next five years and this is the best way I know to do that!" There's a kind of flat finality in my voice, which I hear echoing in my own ears. "It might mean that we have to bring on acquisitions sooner rather than later...I think it's a blessing in disguise that we have to get creative and go off the beaten track to find the right smaller acquisitions."

"What do you think, Rory?"

"It's still a worthy goal and we will be stronger as a company for heading down this road. I don't know if we can increase our profitability by 50% while at the same time doubling the size of our company; for all I know, the divisions may have already picked all the low hanging fruit and that would leave us with all the heavy lifting to do from day one. Even if that proves to be true though and suppose we only achieve 25% growth in EBIT, say 8% to 10%, it will still change the face of this company."

Although Smithy is quiet during all of this he is filled with rapt attention; he is happy to be involved with the senior executive decisions.

"I agree, Rory; the big challenge will be in managing shareholder and board expectations. Even if we got to 10% EBIT and maintained our top line, we could piss off our loyal shareholders and see the company's market cap slip, maybe a lot."

"Growing the top line by an average of 10% per year in the current economic climate will be extremely difficult," says John. "It's not as if the marketplace is growing; we will have to take market share from our competitors, and none of them are going to give it up easily!"

"Or find new markets offshore, and maybe new products too!" says Bill.

"I think it will have to be a combination of all of these things," I say. "Let's get back at it lads and lassies. I hope you have found your lunch break relaxing!"

"This entire exercise has several purposes that include a view of where we want to be in five years' time as compared to where we are now, a reality check as to whether or not we think that will be possible, a vision of the future to weigh our current and future decisions against, and finally a road map to guide us through the required changes year over year."

"So now what we have to do is look at each section from the mission statement right through to the financial implications and if we have not already arrived at this vision, we must determine what we have to do to get there, this list becomes the critical issues we must resolve."

And with no further ado we get at it together.

CRITICAL ISSUES

- Establish a culture that ensures open, honest, and accessible management.
- Establish and phase in a pay for performance/gain sharing system.
- Develop ongoing excellence in continuous improvement.
- Reduce costs and increase value and profit by 1 percentage point per year.
- Develop global excellence in sales.
- Grow the business top line by an average of 10% per year.
- Encourage cross-functional teams at all levels of the business.
- Reward inventiveness; always be on the lookout for new products, services, and markets.
- Get closer/more stickiness with our clients.
- Give better, more inventive pricing and value to our clients.
- Hold ourselves and each other accountable for performance.
- Develop expertise in due diligence.
- Develop expertise in business integration and the achievement of targeted synergies.
- Be prepared to make acquisition prior to the fourth quarter of the fourth year.
- Optimize all existing business performance now.
- Grow our offshore presence for our BPO business.
- Explore and grow our markets globally.
- Consider offshore manufacturing growth.

We review the work we have done together on our strategy. "What do you think guys?"

"I feel a bit better about it after breaking down the bits for action, but I have to tell you I am looking forward to the brainstorming session on acquisitions," says John.

"Me too, John, and yet for some reason, I actually think we just might pull this thing off," says Bill.

"Linda?" I ask.

"I have to say this is the most exciting thing that has ever happened to me in my life! What VP of sales ever was offered such a challenge? I want to get at it!"

"Poor girl doesn't get out much," quips John.

"Rory?" I ask.

"I'm good," says Rory.

"Smithy?"

Smithy seems almost startled to be asked for his opinion by the CEO.

"I think it's great. I love the systematic approach, and with your permission, I'll start breaking the critical issues down into projects. I can leave the start dates on each floating until you determine the relative priority of each issue. And no, I will definitely not involve any of my team yet!"

"Good job, everyone; let's have a short break before we tackle the acquisition strategy. I think we should talk with our communications officer tomorrow and solicit her help on who to involve in this next phase and when it's time to expand the circle a little."

13

Defining the M&A Targets

It's getting late when we finally settle back into work mode, maybe 7.30 p.m. We got burned out at around 6:00 and slipped out to the nearest McDonald's to eat something and to try to get the numbness out of our minds. We looked like a sorry bunch gathered around a couple of tables shoveling our French fries and Big Macs down our throats. The restaurant was busy, lots of people picking up food to take away and a few sitting down to their meals. Most of them seemed to have in common the fact that their workday was over; we envied that. Although we were at least twelve hours into our workday, the most difficult part was still ahead of us.

Only four hours ago I had sprung it on the team that we had to do an about-face with our thinking on acquiring a new business, instead of the luxury of having a broker find a nice big one for us to bid on and fret over. It had become obvious that we would have to do a few smaller ones if we wanted to grow to the desired levels through acquisition, we simply couldn't afford to play…and pay in the big league.

So now here we are, tired and a little dispirited, and yet the called-for state of mind is creative, not discouraged!

"OK," I start, stepping myself up through walking around while adjusting my posture and tonality. "We have to get creative here folks. Rory, get on the pen and draw a map on the flip charts whenever we get on a lucid thread."

Rory is on his feet and he's taping four sheets of flip chart paper together and then fixing the whole thing to the wall.

We start brainstorming ideas that might add synergistically to our four current businesses. The lists are not very long and yet we still can disregard our weakest thoughts in real time. We aren't disrespecting each other; it's just that there are six good brains in the room and that we are a good team and can add to ideas *or* drop them on the fly.

After an hour of this, we have what might be considered slim picking, but it's a start.

Automotive: Add assembly to our parts business, consider an offshore location.

BPO: Build off our automotive technical assistance and customer assistance business, buy an automotive marketing company, and offer a complete suite of BPO offerings to our existing clients and to new clients and geographies. Open a contact center location in the Philippines or India to do call work and back-of-house work for our clients/take advantage of labor arbitrage.

Food and beverage business: Purchase a candy and soft drinks business, purchase a generic pharmaceutical business, introduce a line of vitamins/fish oil capsules, etc.

Metals business: Buy a high-speed packaging company/can plant.

Rory is scribbling down ideas, creating boxes and flow charts, and adding them to our current business searching for a fit; he can hardly keep up with the flow of ideas.

"So what does all of this have in common?" I ask, staring at the map on the wall.

"It's a bloody mess," says John.

"It's disjointing and very busy," says Linda. "How could we manage such a business, it looks like we have no specialty or core competence!"

"Hang on," says Bill. "We are seeing the glass half empty; let's look for what the four businesses and the new ideas have in common and then consider synergies."

"Good, Bill," I say. "Let's do that."

The ideas begin to flow again, and yet again Rory is hard-pressed to keep up:

- The food business uses cans for our current beverage filling line.
- The food business packs soup and vegetables in cans.
- Vitamins and candy bars could help make us a one-stop shop.
- The metals business can buy coils of tin plate and aluminum for our can lines, keeping the profit in house.
- The metals business can sell more partially formed materials to our automotive business, keeping the profits in house.

- We could partner with an offshore automotive assembler in China or Mexico?
- We can ship automotive parts from North America for subassembly offshore and re-import to North America while taking advantage of labor arbitrage.
- The BPO business can offer the same high levels of industry expertise as before to existing and new clients, but with a wider range of products and services and reduced/blended pricing through labor arbitrage.
- The BPO business can partner with our current and new clients to offer services that can be measured against the client's business objectives, e.g., reduce warranty costs for the automotive clients through first time fixes from our technical assistance center as opposed to taking the easy way out and parts changing.

"This is brilliant thinking," I say, "absolutely brilliant!" I look at the complexity of Rory's makeshift organizational map, as does everyone else. "Now, what else does this map tell us; what are the implications and the opportunities for synergies?"

The team is entranced; all signs of fatigue are gone, and you can virtually see the wheels in their brains spinning. They all start shouting out ideas at once; even Rory has given up any pretense of just being the facilitator.

- All the businesses except BPO use transportation for supplies in and goods out.
- There is potential for purchasing assets only in some cases, e.g., the can lines.
- There is potential to partner, reducing acquisition costs.
- Each business can to some degree or other supply their sister companies.
- We have process improvement expertise that goes beyond business content.
- We could purchase businesses that require turnaround, reducing our acquisition costs.
- We should consider buying a transportation company.
- We should consider an internal consulting business and make it available to our external customers at a value price.

We go over the map, make additions, and draw in arrows to identify new synergies and we take a stab at the sales each new acquisition/addition could be expected to add. At the end of the session we have a beautiful map, well, we think it's beautiful, useful at least.

"We have to tidy this up and show it to Alex and see what he thinks," I say. "It should also serve as a road map to brief our acquisition broker when we select one."

Smithy chips in, "The five of us will spend some time and pretty this up for you: Bill for financials, Linda for sales and marketing, John for operations, and Rory to translate the god awful mess he made of the map!"

Rory nods agreement to Smithy; he is smiling ear to ear.

"See you tomorrow, folks," I say. "And thanks; you've been brilliant!"

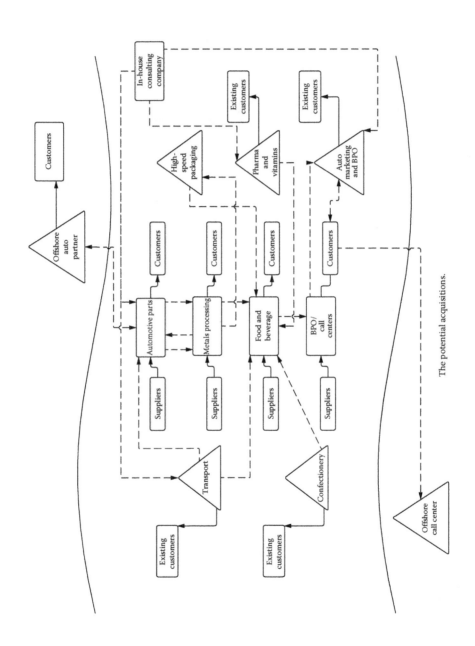

The potential acquisitions.

14

The Business Analysis Training...
Think...Think...Think

"Time is passing and yet we are making good use of it. There's an old adage that states work has the ability to fill the time available. I've seen that axiom prove itself many times but it can't happen here; we will allow a minimum of time between task issuance and update. That works every time too!"

John and I are in the large training room at one of our BPO locations, the output from our service division is completed back office tasks, which have been processed. There is no material output. It is a heavily people-oriented business with ongoing training required to familiarize our people with the ever-changing skills and knowledge required to handle our clients' work content, and so this is where we have the largest training rooms! Today, we have borrowed the room to brief our newly minted analysis team; there are sixteen of them sitting as if in a classroom.

"This will be a fun assignment. You will get a break from your routine job, possibly for several months, and some of you may decide that this line of work will be your chosen profession going forward. There will be times that it proves to be difficult and challenging and there will be times that it will be boring and routine. I urge you to stick with it, you will learn a lot in a short time and these new tools will accompany you for the rest of your working life."

I look at John and he kicks in.

"None of this is rehearsed or preprepared; it's not a recipe, or if it is it's the kind of recipe your old granny used to make her soup for the family, totally experiential. I've known Rory here ever since he was a pup and I trust him completely. I've seen the work he does and the magic he weaves; he admits to it being magic but claims it's everyday magic, the same type his granny used on the soup. This is all very good news, because it means it can be learned and it will be our task to teach you and expose you to as much of its value as possible."

I take the lead again.

"Rule number one: believe everything is possible and that you can change anything! This may not always prove to be true, but it will be true more often than not and it will carry you forward. John is always reminding me that I never show doubt, and that even when I feel it, I simply keep going forward, you should work on doing the same, it's quite a handy trick!"

Our sixteen new analysts are taking notes. That's a very good thing as there will be lots of new stuff to learn and remember over the coming months.

"I'm calling them rules but please don't take that literally or think that this is some kind of sequence. Damn the rules, break the rules, be mavericks, but don't make a big fuss when you do or you'll only make problems for yourself!"

Now the team openly laugh out loud, and I ask them why.

"We've heard about you, Rory; your reputation precedes you. We hear you are a pirate."

"Half of the lies people tell about me are not true." I respond, and continue.

"Rule number two is trust your gut; if something doesn't seem right, it probably isn't. Even if the facts seem clear and yet it still feels wrong, challenge it, either openly or by digging deeper in your own time."

"Rule number three: be nice; it took me a long time to learn that one, and there's no need for you to make the same mistakes I did. If you feel blocked in any way, underreact rather than overreact; you'll still get to the bottom of it. If you can't get around the obstacles, tell John or me; we'll get round them and we'll do it without hanging anyone out to dry. Everyone is doing the job the best way they think they should and you will need the help of all of these good folks before we're done."

A hand goes up, "What if we lose our temper?"

"Apologize," says John. "But don't sweat it; everyone loses their temper. Try not to do it too often though or you'll make it tougher on yourself. And don't waste your time or emotional energy on thinking either Rory or I will judge you harshly when you make mistakes. We've already judged you and found you perfect or you wouldn't be here!"

More laughter.

"Rule number four: begin with the end in mind. Know what you are striving to achieve in every element of your work, in every aspect of analysis, and later in the implementation of every change, fix, and improvement. Sticking with analysis for the moment; it is often like trying to find a needle in a haystack and that's good. As long as you know what the needle you are seeking actually looks like, you will eventually find it. But if you don't know what you are looking for, you might come back with a horseshoe. If you don't understand something, it's because we haven't made it clear enough, so ask John or me for clarification; you will not be a nuisance, not ever. This is our job and we are working with you as one team."

"OK so far?" I ask and the team nods. "I know these things are basic but it's the basics that will carry us through—always remember and practice the basics."

John and I then develop concepts for the analysis on flip charts.

"There are many types of analysis and yet three principal types will gather most of the information you need; these three will culminate in our producing a current state map of how business is done in the area we are analyzing. The three are

1. *Interviews*: The information you seek can be gathered quickly using this method, but remember that this information is subjective. It represents the thoughts and possibly the beliefs of the people you are interviewing. I say possibly the beliefs because some people will lie; it's just the way it is—just like everyone loses their temper...everyone lies, sometimes that is. Know what information you are seeking in advance, formulate your questions and be as unthreatening as possible when you ask people for it. If you like to take notes then do, if you feel more comfortable not taking them you should write down the salient points in your hardbound notebook as soon as possible afterward. I suggest you start with the interview approach.

2. *Data analysis*: There is no end of data available in any business these days. Use the information you get from the interviews to determine where you should dig deeper. Just ask for the info you need, it will already have been cleared with everyone that it should be given to you. Make notes of your conclusions for your reference, always in your hardbound note book. Make a graph showing the data point that particularly interest you so that you can better understand what is happening over time.

3. *Observation*: Go and look at the work being done and confirm that it reflects what you have been told. Make notes where there are stoppages, wasted effort like rework, underutilized capacity and unnecessary movement of product, waiting, and those kinds of things. Go back and ask more questions and look at more data; analysis is circular.

Finally, we will develop a current state map of how we conduct our business in each area, which is under analysis, and if it's perfect and we can't improve on it, our job is done!"

Thank god for a sense of humor, the folks laugh out loud again.

"If it isn't perfect, we will design what could be, we will have it vetted by the management of the business unit and then the employees involved, and then, my dear friends, we will fix it!"

"I am full time on this analysis with you. We will work across the whole company in small teams of between two and four depending on the task at hand. I will be with every team every day. John has a full-time job. He runs the operations of the entire company. He will visit us and we will report out to him, but know that even when he is not in line of site he is on our side."

"We can do this easy!"

"We will work on the analysis in all four businesses consecutively, one core team in each division. We will go through the same paces at each location giving our workmates the core tools they will require and soliciting their involvement in being part of the solution."

"Try not to be driven by any process we show you," I exhort. "Remember that processes are there to help gather and organize information, but they do not replace thinking! So be free; use the process but don't let it use you. Remember, it's the result that we are looking for and remember that in all cases the result is a growth in sales and in profit. The profit will be the easiest to find, the most obvious; it lies in discovering where we can improve how we do things and become more efficient. In the process of becoming more efficient though we will invariably stumble across how to be more effective. Efficiency is doing things right whereas effectiveness is doing the right things; you will recognize the difference between the two with experience and practice."

"In the case of efficiency gains, you will find them in wasted activity, sequence of activity, waiting time, errors and rework, set up times, that sort of stuff. In the case of effectiveness, it will surface as unused time, holes, and gaps of hours that can be utilized to increase throughput whether in the guise of people deployment or equipment utilization. These gaps are the future gateway to profitable increased sales; they will open up opportunities for our sales folks to sell additional products at competitive prices because our fixed assets and costs will already be covered in the sales price of existing products."

"A major point to be looking out for, and I can't stress it enough, is what I call finding the *nut*. The nut isn't really a nut at all, but it's useful to think of it that way. It is the core issue that has to be cracked to open the way for us to reach our overall goals in productivity and in throughput, which of course will create our increased profit and sales goals at the manufacturing level."

"The normal sequence of the discovery of opportunities for improvement is to uncover a host of seemingly unrelated things that we can improve, and this is good so go after this. At some point though, whether by a blinding flash of the obvious or by long hard thinking and discussion, we will find *the nut*, the central concept, problem, or opportunity that if focused upon and cracked will affect everything else for the better. It's like the old saying *all roads lead to Rome*! It's around this nut that we will establish the majority of our core productivity control systems. The nut can be a different thing in every environment or business unit; it can be different in sales, inventory control, or manufacturing. Don't let that fact frighten you. We will find the nuts to crack right across the company and we will crack them; processes will help with this but thinking will be the final breakthrough, it always is."

"For now, though I would like you to work at unearthing opportunities through analysis and through logging what you see, each of your teams has a leader and each morning you should meet to discuss the tactics of the day, who goes where looking for what. Each evening you should close the day with a half-hour meeting to share what you have found. Keep all your information and findings in your hardbound note books, no loose leaf or ring tabs, and consolidate the info on flip charts at your evening meetings."

"I will be in each location once every four days at which time you can bring me up to date, and then I'll spend the rest of my time with you working on your specific project. I will, however, call each leader every day to see if you need any help."

I go over the basic steps in each analysis approach:

Interviews

Be respectful.

Feel free to ask whichever questions come to mind and use the following as guidelines.

- What exactly do you do here?
- What are your productivity targets?
- What are your quality targets?
- What is your productivity achievement as compared to target?
- What is your quality achievement as compared to target?
- What are the biggest problems you face in achieving productivity and quality targets?
- Do you have any recurring problems?
- Are there any people problems? What are they?
- How is performance rewarded?
- Do you have a problem resolution process? What is it?
- If you could do three things differently in your department, what would they be?
- If you do nothing different, what will your business look like in a year's time?
- What's the difference between a good day and a bad day?

Data analysis

- Analyze the financial data.
- Analyze the productivity and quality data.
- Analyze the problem resolution process.
- Analyze lateness and absenteeism.
- Analyze downtime and production logs.

Look for patterns and inconsistencies, does one product have more scrap or rework? Does one shift perform better than others? Is there more downtime in one area/machine than others?

Observation analysis

- Look at the entire production/process flow as one entity.
- Always make notes of your observations.

- Put the time in the margin frequently, down to the minute if you can.
- Identify key points in the process and observe them in detail, minimum 2 hours per area. Always with the short interval time in the margin.
- Identify waste in any of its guises.
- Look at the same process across different shifts.
- Ask questions around any problems that you see (ask operators, supervisors, setters).
- Analyze, validate, and consolidate your findings.

"On my first physical visit with each team, we will begin building a current state process map based on the information we have at that time. We will continue with this approach right through each division and on through the entire company, and then we will build the future state map together, always ensuring we keep all of the key stakeholders in the company up to date."

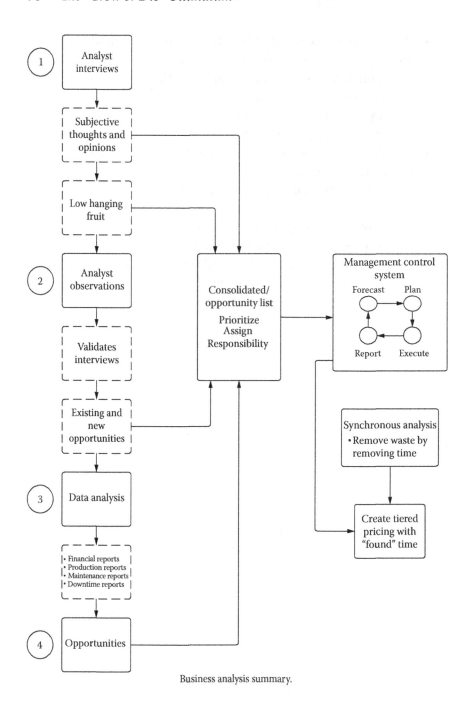

Business analysis summary.

15

Selecting the Right Broker

It's time to find the right intermediary, the broker who will represent us in the search for the right business to acquire.

"Hi, Alex, it's James. How are you this fine morning?"

"I'm good, James, and you? How is our little venture progressing?"

"I'd love to feel self-assured enough to call it a little venture, Alex, but I would say it's right on track. Is this a good time for you to talk?"

"Yes, we are just finishing up a meeting here and my part in it is done. I'll wander down to my office and call you back in five minutes, OK?"

"That would be great, thanks Alex."

True to his word, my phone rings in exactly five minutes.

"So what can I do for you, James?"

"You recall telling me that you had three guys in mind that could potentially help us as an intermediary in our search for the right acquisition? Well I think it's time old friend."

"I do remember, James, and less of the old if you don't mind, soon you will notice that time skips by very quickly for all of us. And it wasn't three guys, it was one woman and two guys."

"Even better. How do you feel we should proceed?"

"I think we should do it in stages, kind of the same approach you have used in gating each step in your overall growth plan. Have you narrowed your search criteria enough to turn a broker loose on the search and does the criteria match your strategy for growth over the next five years?"

"We have narrowed the search criteria and we have taken steps to reflect the changes the growth plans have on our five-year strategy. We would like to run them past you when you have time, Alex."

"Does tomorrow afternoon suit you, James?"

"It does, Alex; it always delights me how quickly you respond to our needs!"

"Well, it's true that I have other business interests James, but none of them are so important that I wouldn't drop them in a heartbeat to come and spend time working with you and your team."

"Thanks, Alex. Oh, one other thing. Could you help us with your thoughts on the criteria we should consider to ensure we have the right intermediary?"

"I already shared my thoughts with you, James; do you recall?"

"I do, Alex, and we have them. I was just wondering if there are any additions or further emphasis you might like to go over with us during your visit."

"I'll jot down some thoughts and fax it to your office, James, but the final selection criteria should be yours and your teams."

"Thanks again, Alex. You suggested that we should gate the steps in the selection of the broker; could you send me your thoughts on that too?"

"Of course, James, I'll fax them along with my additional thoughts on the broker selection; see you tomorrow around 1:00 p.m.?"

"I look forward to it, Alex."

Twenty minutes later, the fax arrives with the two lists:

Broker selection criteria

- Good knowledge of industry targeted
- Good track record in acquisitions in the $300 million range
- Superior people skills
- At least fifteen years' experience as an acquisitions intermediary
- Great references
- Cost structure/fee schedule in line with the industry
- Paid only if they introduce the acquisition, not if it comes across the transom
- Cut-off period of two years to present an acquisition that fits our criteria

Gated steps to hiring a broker

- Review selection criteria with executive team and refine list.
- Review strategy and acquisition criteria with board.
- Individual interviews with each senior executive (CEO, COO, CFO).
- Interview with chairman of the board.
- Group interview with all four above parties.
- Preliminary selection.
- Reference checks.
- Final selection.

16

Initial Internal Analysis Findings

The guys and the ladies have been doing good work on the analysis in all four divisions; they've been at it for two weeks now, and I've talked with them every day either by conference call or during personal visits. I'm generally happy with what I see, and they are generally as nervous as kittens! The combination of good work so far and the team's nervousness has got me thinking that we need to get together again as an entire team to review progress to date, and so we meet at head office in the boardroom. It's a full house—all sixteen of the analysis team plus James, John, Bill, and Smithy...and me, of course. The head office team is brilliant; they show and express total commitment for what the team is doing. We have a full and busy day ahead of us, and James kicks it off.

"Hi, everyone. How many people in the room has met me in person before today?" Three out of the sixteen analysis team members raise their hands. "That makes me feel terrible, folks; I try to get around the business as often as I can and clearly it's not often enough. I'll do better, I promise."

I chip in, "Don't be so hard on yourself, James. You're doing a fine job and the guys know it." There's lots of nodding of approval in the room.

"Thanks for that, guys, and thanks to you, Rory, but it is my avowed intent to do better! I hope today is some evidence of that...what you are spearheading right now is the future of our company and all of us are with you, today and every day, please know that. Call me, talk to me, I'll be highly available, and when I'm not I'll get back to you next day. I may not always be able to tell you everything that's going on, but I promise I will never lie to you, and I will keep you up to date on everything as soon as I am able to. You have this same promise from Rory and John and from Bill and Smithy. Rory has kept me up to speed on progress so far and I'm excited to see what we will cover today."

With that James nods to me and I continue.

"We have a lot to get through, guys, so let's get at it. I'm going to jot a few main headings on the flip chart and you can help me fill in the blanks. We'll use this as a working agenda for the day and go through all of the items together. It's my hope that at the close of day we will have consolidated the analysis findings from across the company, highlighted any behavioral issues, and come up with an immediate action plan that we can start implementing alongside further and ongoing analysis. So let's begin."

I move to the flip chart and begin to write.

- Gather bullet point info from the interview studies conducted in each division.
- Gather info on low-hanging fruit opportunities from each division.
- Discuss and record the most salient points from observation studies.
- Discuss and study most salient points from data analysis.
- Discuss any behavioral issues.
- Introduce the concept of managing the performance system.
- Introduce the concept of four-point planning.
- Go into depth on how to find "the nut," the core issues related to improving the business in each area.
- Gather all of the threats and opportunities into a project plan for resolution.
- Determine next steps.

We sweat over this list together and the team gets uncomfortable, while James, John, and Bill get increasingly interested. For Smithy's part, there is a never-ending flurry of note-taking.

"The objective here, guys, is to boil down the information you have gathered. If we are persistent in our determination to boil down each element we examine in each business, and then talk about the things that we may have observed but were not told, and the things our intuition tells us, we will find similarities in the several nuts we have to crack to move the entire business forward."

Uneasiness is a very interesting thing, a palpable thing, and it fills the room, and yet as a team we have to proceed through it to get the result, step by step.

Tony begins with the metals division, "The interviews told us this":

- Everyone is afraid from senior management down; it seems like we are looking under the covers.
- No one wants to name names as to who is creating blocks, but they make it obvious through where the blocks are actually happening.
- There has been a comfort level regarding performance that has led to stagnation.
- Everyone needs support in going forward into change; they need a get-out-of-jail-free card for having fallen asleep at the wheel.

Tony continues, "When we combine the information from our on-the-floor observations with the information we found in analyzing the data and reports, we find some very obvious parallels."

- Downtime on the floor is taken for granted and accepted as the norm.
- Day-to-day performance is considered fine if it falls within previous norms.
- People are afraid to point the finger at each other for performance discrepancies.
- There is no process for finding the root causes for recurring problems.
- There are obvious possible causes that could lead to the root causes of problems and help us find the nut.
- The production reports and downtime reports are disconnected and unused.
- The various departments work in silos.
- There is duplication and waste in each location's inventory due to a lack of policy regarding sharing.

There is a stunned silence in the room from everyone as these items fall onto the flip chart and into the light of day. I encourage each team from each division to talk about their findings and we find each to be remarkably similar in what has been found.

Finally, James breaks the silence, "Can we fix this?" All of the heads in the room nod the affirmative.

James continues in a non-threatening and supportive tone, "Do you know how to fix it?"

"Knowing and doing are two very different things," says Brian, the lead analysis from the automotive division.

James, Bill, and John nod in agreement to this obvious truth and look at me; everyone is looking at me!

"How do you eat an elephant?" I ask.

The whole room laughs and jeers at me, and the pregnant silence is gone as they chant out the answer they have heard a thousand times already, "One bite at a time!"

"We need structure," I say. "In all of our endeavors toward improvement, we always need structure. The various processes that we will use are just that, processes that give our efforts structure. There's nothing magic about them. They are all based on common sense, and they are not the only valid methods that would move us forward. Generally speaking, any good process will work. We will select tried and true methods and approaches that will move us toward consistency and results; it's like having a toolbox and applying the right tool to each task. Each approach will interlock with the others just like a jigsaw, and when the final piece is slotted into place, we will have a picture of not only where we are but also where we are going and how we are going to get there. We will also have triggers that will constantly cause us to take the required actions and ensure constant follow-up."

It's John's turn to speak, "Well that's a load off my mind, Rory!" and the room laughs again! "I'm not being facetious pal. I've seen the results of your approach before and I know you will stay the course through it with us!"

The sandwiches and cold cans of pop arrive and we have a working lunch, after which we continue through the four divisions to arrive at specific companywide and divisional lists.

Next we ask each team to brainstorm low-hanging fruit opportunities; we don't do this a division at a time but roll through it as a general discussion. John, James, Bill, and Smithy join in with their thoughts, even I chip in, which is a bit of a no-no for the facilitator, but I have the experience to add, and goddamn it, I'm adding. It's brilliant when the list is large, significant, and diverse and this list certainly is. We have not second guessed any item and instead have freely built upon them, often with various individuals chipping in on each issue.

"So listen, guys, we have to break this down further to make it actionable, let's do it in three steps. First we will go over the lists, eliminate duplicates, and combine issues where they relate to the same problem or potential solution. Next, we will prioritize this shorter list for action both corporately and divisionally, and then we will determine if there is a logical sequence of events and who should take primary responsibility for the completion of each task with a start date and projected end date. Oh… and the fourth of our three steps should be how much money we hope to save as a target for each initiative. Let's get at it."

At the close of the exercise, we have the following opportunity list for the low-hanging fruit:

- Eliminate the cost of duplicate inventory in the various locations in the metals business.
- Eliminate the cost of premium freight in the auto business.
- Fix recurring stop–start problems in the food processing and packing lines.
- Reduce attrition in the BPO group.
- Increase accountability for output performance in all divisions.
- Improve on-time delivery in the metals division.
- Reduce set-up and changeover time in the auto group.
- Improve coaching and training effectiveness in BPO.
- Improve throughput in known bottlenecks in the food-processing business.
- Identify bottlenecks and remove them company wide.
- Reduce work in process (WIP) to a working but effective minimum company wide.
- Create staging areas for next-day deliveries companywide.
- Maximize on the usage of pull systems for products companywide.
- Improve die reliability between runs in auto.
- Reduce changeover times throughout the business.
- Improve occupancy and staffing levels in BPO.
- Focus on customer satisfaction companywide.
- Stop overproducing into the warehouses.
- Ensure the management is on the floor actively managing.
- Ensure the necessary tools and direction are in place for the operators.
- Ensure there are systems in place to identify and resolve problems in real time companywide.
- Reward and recognize superior performance.
- Eliminate fear.

We then add opportunities by division from the findings generated by the observations, again prioritizing and sequencing and assigning primary responsibility as we did with the low-hanging fruit. Smithy is working feverishly on the combined lists to form the initial outline of a project plan; I have to tell you I am really impressed by this, young man!

"Can you knock that out by the end of the day, Smithy?" I ask. He simply nods and leaves the table with his laptop.

"You're going to get resistance! I say again to be clear on that, we are all going to get resistance! We all have personal power outside of our roles in the company, and that's not just true for us but for those who will resist us too. We have to overcome the resistance and we will do that by staying together as a team." In saying this, I nod to James and John.

"I've told you I'm in," says James, "and I am, 100%! Don't judge me by what I say but by what I do; you will see I am truly a 100 percenter."

"Me too," says John.

"So, it seems that we already recognize we are having people problems, particularly with the senior folks within your own divisions," I say. "Why do you think that is?"

The answers are slow in coming at first and then come in an avalanche and I begin to capture them.

- They are afraid.
- They don't want you to see under the covers.
- There may be more problems than even they know about.
- They will be considered failures.
- They may lose their jobs.
- They don't want to look like fools.
- They don't want to look like they have been doing nothing.

The list goes on, but this captures the essence of it.

"Do you think their fears are justified?" I ask.

By the nods and murmurs, clearly everyone thinks they are.

"I want to make something clear," says James. "Any failures that the division heads may have are mirrored in the performance of John and I, we are responsible for the performance and goings on in every division. All of these guys report to us one way or another and if we haven't controlled what's going on the buck stops at us, that's how the chain of command is supposed to work, and so we are not finger pointing here. Rory, tell us how we can get around this."

"Well, all of these reasons for resistance seem to be based on fear, we have to eliminate that fear and make it clear that it's a new day. Everything happens in its time and today must be seen as a new start, a clean sheet and a get-out-of-jail-free card for everyone. That is so long as they haven't broken any laws and get on board taking the current performance as the new baseline from which we will springboard into the future. It seems to me that this is not an option, so we should meet with them again and James will make that clear."

James nods his agreement, "We will do that when we present the consolidated findings of this analysis."

I continue, "Once that is clear" we will set up a new performance management system that triggers the necessary performance and behaviors we need, and that rewards the right behaviors while discouraging those behaviors that are not conducive toward meeting the new goals. This will be for all of us...including the senior leadership."

"It will require a bit of work but its structure is easy to follow, you could say it's quite simple and yet we have to remember simple and easy are two very different things. The concept is simple; the implementation takes consistent follow-up and no small amount of backbone," I say. "Let's look at the elements."

1. Set and agree the expected performance targets.
2. Determine which behaviors are needed to achieve the targets.
3. Determine the frequency of the review periods.
4. Set up consequences that support the appropriate behaviors and discourage the inappropriate behaviors.
5. Revisit the achievement of the expected performance targets to ensure the appropriate behaviors are moving us toward them, and the consequences are supporting the appropriate behaviors and discouraging their opposite.
6. Adjust as necessary.

"We will formalize this into a document covering each of the six elements as they relate to every level of the organization, and as long as we ensure our follow-up and any necessary adjustments, it will form a steel chain of appropriate behaviors and results throughout the organization with each link supporting the next in line. We should follow this up at all levels every three months during our formal reviews, although in truth, the results will trigger follow-up every day in real time!"

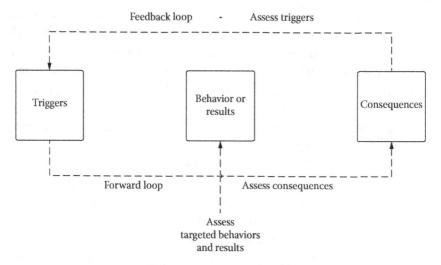

Performance management model.

17

Four-Point Planning

The teams are all here, including James, John, and the rest of the boys from the head office.

"We need to discuss four-point planning, I know we have talked about it before and yet we have to go deeper. Some of the reasons why it's so powerful include that it helps us consolidate our analysis during the construction of the current state map, and then allows us to create a future state map by identifying and eliminating any disconnects and areas of poor performance in how we do things now. It also acts as a great visual tool to encourage us to gather needed information and changes from all of the stake holders in the process under study."

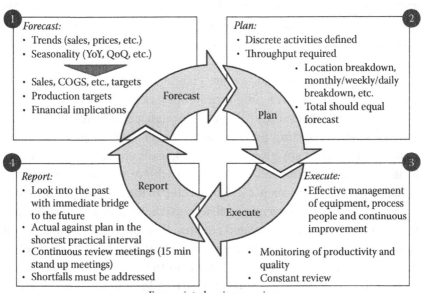

Four-point planning overview.

"The four elements are Forecast—Plan—Execute—Report. Of course, we do all of these things now, but often the elements don't serve the business as well as they could, and equally importantly, they may be disconnected from each other allowing major problems or opportunities to go unnoticed in real time!" This discussion is obviously ringing a few bells, as people are leaning forward, nodding, murmuring, and taking notes... good, they're still awake!

"I've worked with some brilliant people in my life who simply hate this process and think it's unnecessary. They make for a hard audience but I've never given up on them, and even although provoked, most have never given up on me!"

"We have to forecast our workload right across the business or we won't know our future build by category, how we must load our staffing and facilities, what it will all cost us, and what our profit will be. Any shortfall in our performance or accuracy here will show up pretty quickly in our P&L and if not fixed in our annual report!"

"We have to plan our workload, or we won't know how much of each category of the total years build should be run today, tomorrow, next week, and next month. If we do not do this effectively, we will have overruns showing up in our inventory or a shortage of supply to meet our customers' needs. We also need to know what level of production has to be met every hour so that we know the difference between a good hour and a bad one and don't simply accept any performance shortfalls as inevitable. If we highlight them as they happen, it will help drive us to fix the problems that cause these shortfalls in real time!"

"Executing our workload is a representation of what we actually do and how we do it. It allows us to fine-tune our processes, our staffing, etc., and to identify the probable cause of any performance shortfalls."

"Finally, our reporting process should be more than just how many units we produce in any given time period; it should be a trigger and call to action for any production shortfalls. To achieve this, we should always report our actual performance in relationship to the planned performance, not in a vacuum. In the event of such a shortfall, we should find and action the most probable cause. If we don't do this, then the problems will persist, as will the shortfalls. A problem or shortfall that could have been resolved in an hour can become repetitive and ruin the entire year's budget, and James will end up explaining and apologizing for it to the board of directors and eventually the shareholders. That's not a pretty sight, is it, James?"

"No, it most certainly is not," says James. "Show us how we can avoid these pitfalls, Rory!"

I go back to the generic four-point planning map and explain again the possibility of disconnects and their resulting shortfalls. "Do we all understand this so far?" I ask.

Everyone signals the affirmative.

"Intellectual knowing is not enough though, folks," I say. "It's in the doing that the true learning takes place."

"What I am going to show you now is a current state map that our team sitting with us from our BPO business put together, which is typical of our current call center business."

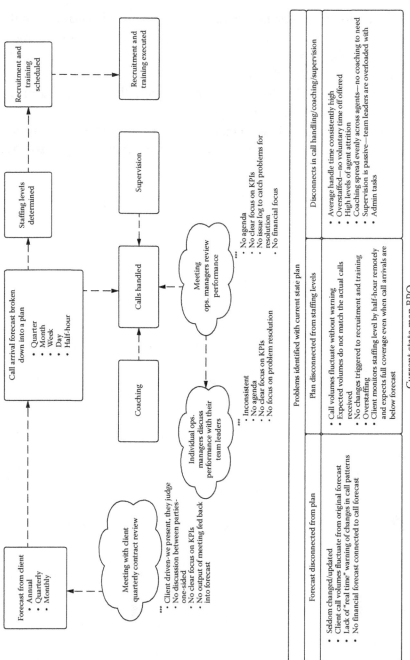

Current state map BPO.

I show the current state map. "Stand up and take a bow, folks!" I encourage, and led by Roberta, the four analysis team members from our BPO business take a bow, half nervously and half proudly.

"Can I ask you to explain what you found please?" I ask encouragingly.

"Well," Roberta responds. "It actually all looks pretty normal until you study it, so we studied it. And studied it and studied it. We had the company's senior and middle management study it too, and we also had the schedulers, supervisors, and agents study it, and lo and behold it was full of disconnects that were contributing to performance shortfalls in the business. You can see where we identified them on the current state map, just follow the dotted lines that highlight the disconnects."

Now everyone in the room is paying attention, some taking notes.

"Continue please," I ask.

"After our analysis of the current state map and its disconnects, we begun to assemble a second map of what things could look like, the future state map. I'm afraid we had to rely heavily on Rory's support in creating this one. It helps to have someone by your side who has done the thing before."

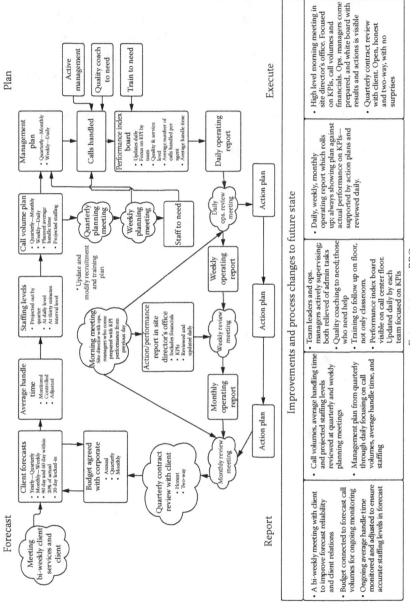

Future state map BPO.

I show the team the future state map, now everyone is paying attention and comparing the current state map to the future state map.

I encourage the team leader to continue.

"The next step was to turn the future state map into a management control system, we could visualize this from the future state map...and through ongoing jabs from Rory, we created and positioned the short interval controls."

"Explain how you did that please," I encourage.

"We looked for the key measures of success for the business, those that if achieved would ensure our qualitative and quantitative targets were met, and that through their achievement our financial targets would also be met, and then we set up our control systems around those key measures."

"Thanks, Roberta," I say, and the team finally sits down. There is actually a round of genuine applause in the room.

I continue to round out the presentation, "So the team designed a series of short daily meetings to compare the actual performance achieved against the target, all reviewing the previous day on each of the key measures." I show these meetings on the future state map. "The team managers meet with the site directors for the review of their teams' performance one after the other and identify the reasons for any shortfall if they exist. They also identify the action that they will take to ensure the problem issue will not arise again tomorrow; the idea is to resolve all problems in real time."

I show a copy of a current Plan against Actual control report with its related problem identification and resolution document.

Plan	Actual	Action Item	Responsibility	Target Date

Plan against actual control report.

You could hear a pin drop in the room. "Tell us what the results are so far in the business please, Roberta."

"After only one week since installation of the new controls, all of the key measures are improving and the business is running more smoothly. Everyone fully expects to see the performance improvement reflected in our financial performance at the end of the month."

The silence in the room turns to applause again.

"What other controls have you put in place around these key measures, Roberta?" I ask.

"We check these same key measures right down to the individual team level. The team manager conducts a fifteen-minute stand-up meeting with the group of their respective team leaders. They check the same measures by team and capture the reason for any shortfalls and the fixes that will be put in place to ensure those same problems will not recur tomorrow."

"Why is it a stand-up meeting?" I ask.

"The team leaders are busy, there is no room for time wasting when the group stands up and reviews the performance in the aisle, and also the teams see the importance of their respective performance. When the meeting is finished, each team's performance is posted on a board on the call center floor."

"So what did this analysis team do?" I ask the room at large.

"They found the nut!" James says.

18

At the Heart of Every Problem There Is a Nut to Crack

The executive team have excused themselves after expressing their delight and giving their stamp of approval to the work conducted by the BPO team on their analysis on the current state four-point planning map and the creating of an improved future state map and management control system that has already begun to achieve results. The team has taken fifteen minutes for a toilet break and to grab some refreshments.

"OK, folks, are we all sitting comfortably?"

"Yes," the team roars. But I know I am wearing them out.

"You folks are doing great work and I know you must be mentally exhausted today. My intent was to go deeper in covering the behavioral aspect of our work, but we can continue with that another day if you like. There's no point in forging ahead if I've got you to the point of being brain dead."

The team laughs, "We want to go ahead, Rory. Are you too tired to do it today, and are you getting old?"

"Not in this lifetime!" I shoot back.

And together we develop one behavioral template each for the COO, divisional presidents, and each of their direct reports within the management structure. The template shows the role for each specific individual, the required behavior, the desired result, and the triggers to ensure the desired behavior happens; the consequence column is left blank and will be determined at each quarterly review.

Divisional President:	Date:			
Triggers	Behavior/Results	Consequences	Self-review	Manager review
• Salary mirrors results • Bonus mirrors results • Performs well in blind 360 performance reviews by employees	• Supportive of all employees • Achieve divisional results • Ensure short interval reports and actions are used • Actively support strategic initiatives • Manages by walking about	Positive results: • Salary and bonus recognition • Employee, peer and superior recognition Negative results: • Recognized in remuneration • Cautions • Performance management	Assess out of 10 on: • Behavior • Results • Write comments on	

Example management performance system chart using divisional president.

The questions flow out from the team, "But isn't every three months for a review too often?"

"No…we are under time pressure to achieve performance improvement and to ensure any necessary process and cultural change, and so we have to constantly check our progress and adjust our aim."

"Then isn't three months too wide of a period?"

"Maybe…but it's better than annually and during the interval between formal reviews there should be consistent review and follow-up all down the line."

"Some managers may be too strict or too lax, or lavish for that matter with the consequences. How do we manage that?"

"At the end of the day, doing the right things is as important as getting the right results. We don't want to see brutality and neither do we want to see the ignoring of issues where corrective action should have been taken. In each formal review, the reviewer will go over the form as filled out by the person being reviewed to ensure they agree with each other, and if the consequence for behavior is deemed not appropriate either for the positive or negative, it will be addressed and changed."

There is still a degree of uncertainty in the room after we have gone over the charts for the senior executives. "What's troubling you, guys?" I ask.

"What about the behavior of the supervisors, and for that matter the operators and other folks on the floor who actually do the job? How will we handle that?"

"Create similar maps for each level to be reviewed by the direct supervisor of everyone involved," I say.

"Work in your existing teams with heavy involvement from human resources using the example of the executive review process as your model and create one process review in each team for whichever level in your division you choose. Make the work visible on a flip chart and be prepared to present it to the group in thirty minutes."

The four teams each move into a different corner of the room, each supported by a human resources specialist and work on creating behavioral maps on their own.

True to form, they are ready to present in thirty minutes. We now have behavioral maps for an operator, a supervisor, a mechanic, and a material handler. The work is solid, they get it, and they know what they are doing!

"Good work, folks," I say. "If we intend to change the face of our organization, we need a culture that is conducive to high performance. James, John, Linda, and I will ensure this is installed at the executive level and I will work with you and human resources to ensure we design and install it properly throughout the organization."

"It would be a good day's work if we stop now; I'm getting tired."

"Brighten up, old man," they jibe at me. "We still have questions."

"Shoot!" I say.

"You talk about focusing on the nut all the time, Rory; can you clarify what you mean by that?"

"Yes of course, I would be pleased to, and it is of course about time." I move over to the flip chart and bullet point the salient points as I am talking.

"The nut to be cracked can be different at every level of the business, department, process, project, and initiative. In almost every case in any organization that is 'for profit,' the nut tends to be financial. At the level of our entire initiative, the nut is to achieve $2 billion in sales at a 12% EBIT."

The questions come from all over the room.

"That equates to $240 million profit! What if we hit the profit target through better margins than 12% but miss the top-line sales of $2 billion?"

"Good question. Worse things could happen; however, the street and our shareholders want to see top-line growth as well as profit growth and so the nut includes both numbers."

"How do we at the shop floor level relate to such a huge overreaching target?"

"I think awareness is first, and our talking about it together creates that awareness. Some of you have told me you have never been involved in discussions of this type before, and so, communication will play a big part in our success. However, our communication must be well thought out; a message misunderstood will always turn out to be the wrong message and so it must be tailored to our audience. There's no secret about where we want to go though, so the message must be truthful and consistent with the end goal."

"How can a production foreman or a line operator relate to this goal so that they can work toward it?"

"By our clearly defining the output required by the process, production line, machine, or individual and triggering the right behavior for its achievement and then setting up consequences that will encourage the continuation of the achievement of the results required from that particular process or individual."

"What if a machine breaks down, or some other unavoidable factor causes downtime?"

"Then we'll catch it through short interval reporting in our four-point plan and we'll put a permanent fix in place."

"It sounds as though all these things fit together and that they are actually one and the same thing. Is that right?"

"Yes it is, and that's where the strength lies."

"So can we get back to the nut please, Rory?"

"Yes of course. The nut is a simple idea but that doesn't make it easy to do. It is always financial in nature but isn't always measured financially; in fact it is measured differently depending on the level of the business it is being addressed at. Let's look at a few examples."

"If the nut is profit dollars being measured by executives in the business and for any reason they are off target you follow the tree down through sales $ and profit % to find the shortfall. If it's sales dollars you determine where the problem is, a specific district or a specific buyer or a specific sales team? You continue boring down until you find root cause and then you fix it! If it's profit %, you do the same thing, you bore down. Did someone discount the price? Are the direct costs or indirect costs above budget? We continue to bore down until we find root cause and then we fix it!"

"The trick is we never quit; we continue to bore down; find the cause, then assume, and demand that we fix it. The nut is the initial link in the chain that when compromised demands the bore down and so that's where you apply your focus and short interval reporting, you always start at the nut! If the nut takes us down to the same link in the chain that is failing repeatedly, we will also install short interval reporting and resolution at that point in the process. The nut prevents the need to focus and then short interval report on every step of every process at all times, if the actual performance at the nut is equal or better than the planned performance, you can move to the next issue without applying time and resources in digging deeper. If the results are significantly above the plan we will dig deeper to find cause; we simply won't be able to help ourselves, but that's the exception. Our planned output tends to be based on required sales for the product or our throughput capacity capability."

I then go through some diverse examples at various levels in the business or process chain and note them on the flip chart.

- In retail, the nut can be sales made per person hour applied and sales dollar per sale. This is true in a video store or a clothes shop or a fast food joint: "would you like fries with that?" There are natural upsells that create a bargain for the customer and properly positioned they almost sell themselves. Right staffing and right activity and scheduling of staff to meet busy periods combined with modest upsells on each ticket can yield millions of dollars in added profit over a year.
- In a call center technical assistance unit for computer support, internet support, and a host of other applications, the nut is the average handle time of the call and the service level. How many of the incoming calls are handled within our targeted maximum wait time? Often the skills for problem resolution will be very specialized with only a proportion of the entire call center group having the primary skill or even language capability. Interlinking groups can be set up and programmed so that the calls are answered by a live agent who can at least progress the call and then message the details of the problem to the agents in the primary group for a call back when the current workload for that group dies down. The final resolution calls will likely be more efficient and much shorter because the agent is preprepared to address the issue and also doesn't have to calm down an angry customer who has been waiting in queue for an extended period.
- In metal distribution, the nut can be many different things, or there can be many different nuts; they can include warehouse throughput—what blocks or impedes the picking, processing or shipping of an item? Process time—what can delay an order from being processed? Inventory cost and availability—what can you carry in stock? What is its replacement cost? How can you best access the item? Sales—how do you measure the team and the individual performance?

- In manufacturing, there can be glaring nuts like the time it takes for a tool change, or equipment reliability, or inventory and shipping. If you are paying a premium to have orders shipped to meet on-time commitments, you can find root cause of many other problems by boring down to eliminate the causes of premium shipment costs.

> To ensure all parts are shipped on time and in full every time, we must identify any causes of delays in short intervals. This will lead us to address problems in the offending areas, thus fixing the entire operation

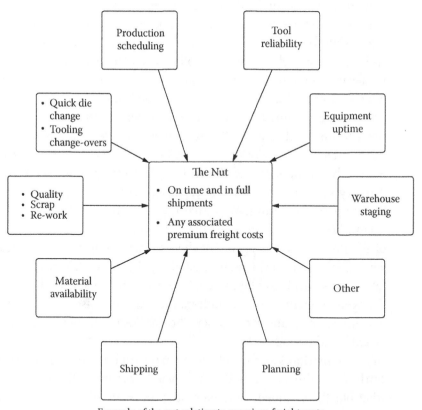

Example of the nut relating to premium freight costs.

"In essence the nut has the characteristic of being the main area or item of focus, which will highlight problems to be resolved to ensure we can achieve our targeted performance level. It is usually connected to all of the other related problems we are experiencing and, therefore, its resolution is often reflected in an improvement of all of the outputs we are striving to achieve. If you get the nut right and you crack it, you will move toward meeting the overall business objectives; however, it is not a one hit wonder. It is around the nut that our primary performance control systems should be set up. What does our hourly, daily, weekly, monthly, and annual plan for the output through the nut require as a quantifiable number of units and does the actual number of units correspond to this expectation or better? Focusing on the reason for any shortfall and eliminating its cause is how we crack the nut."

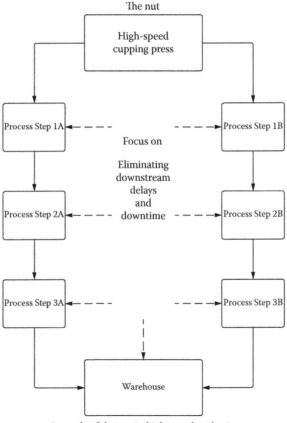

Example of the nut in high-speed packaging.

19

Corporate Culture

John and I have called the four division presidents into head office to discuss the progress of the analysis so far. To speak generally, they seem subdued, and yet it seems crucial that I, as CEO, should be the main bearer of this particular message.

First John brings them up to date on the findings of the analysis across the company; their manner becomes even quieter than before when they see the consistency of "the fear factor."

John finishes his presentation and I pick the pace up, "Does it surprise any of you that there is fear in your management teams?"

Tony Dent of the food division kicks in first, "There's fear in any business; it depends on the individual, and let's face it when consultants and your own team mates are poking their heads under the covers. It can be a bit alarming."

John takes it head on with Dave Mason, "Are you scared, Dave? Are your people scared?"

Dave lets out a chuckle, "There's not that much that scares me any more, John. I don't want to be in a job where I'm not capable or wanted, and so it's OK for you to prepare a package for me if I'm not the right guy for the job!"

"Is that what you want?" I ask.

"No, it certainly is not, James. I guess I got a little defensive there."

"What about your management team, Dave. Do they have any reason to be afraid?"

"I'm a bit demanding on them and have lost my temper from time to time," says Dave.

"What about your team in BPO, Jennifer?" asks John. "Any fear there?"

"There sure is," responds Jennifer, "in me and everyone else."

"Why is that?" I ask.

"My division is delivering the poorest financial performance in the entire company," she responds. "Given that we are not even achieving the budget, how would you expect us to feel when that basic target level is being increased by 50%? People are afraid for their jobs, James!"

"What about you, Harry? How are things in auto?" asks John. "Any fear in your management team?"

"I think it's fair to say that some of the lads are concerned," says Harry. "The way we manage is under scrutiny by Rory and our own people who are working with him. We have been managing the business in the same old way for years and now it doesn't seem that it's enough anymore. It looks like we are managing by consensus and none of us are used to that."

"And your team at foods, Tony?" asks John.

"I'm fine," says Tony defensively, "but some of my senior team are getting a bit agitated."

"Why is that?" I ask.

"Well, we are the strongest performing division in the company, and all of a sudden, it seems it's not good enough!"

"It's not," I say. "None of our performance is good enough; the game has changed. We have a new prime objective and that's to grow our core business by 33% and our profits 50%! We've gone over that together and we are moving toward it…together."

There is complete silence in the room.

"I need you to understand that even after we achieve the required growth in our core business it is not over; it will never be over. We intend to go on the acquisition trail; the company will grow by another 50% after we've achieved our current goals. The demands on your skills and on the skills of your teams will be tested even further."

It's hard to imagine how silence can deepen, but it just did, although this time with different flavors of interest, kind of multifaceted. Some of the folks seem fascinated and others frightened.

"I need to know you are on board," I say. "All of our jobs are going to get bigger and I need a strong team with me, a committed team. If you can't be part of that team, let John or I know and we will find someone who can."

I don't normally come across so forcibly, but there's a point to be made here.

"Dave, are you in?"

"Sure am, boss," Dave responds.

"Harry?"

"For sure, it's exciting!"

"Jennifer?"

"I am, but I'll need a lot of help."

"Good," I respond. "We will work on all of this together."

"Tony?"

"Yes," he responds.

"Good," I say. "It's a new day, in monopoly they call it a get-out-of-jail-free card and that's what I'm offering everyone today, all of our people. I know we have the right team here to get this done and as long as no one has broken the law, then we all have a clean slate. I want you and your teams to know it's a new day and there's no need for anyone to be afraid; fear is corrosive. I need you to boost your team's morale; help me create a new culture where we hold each other accountable while still respecting each other. If we can't do that in our existing business, we have no chance once we begin acquiring others.

Welcome the help you get from Rory and the teams he has built from your people; work with them proactively. Make ours the company we all know it can be!"

20

The Project Plan

Now we will review the project plan for the next five years with a heavy focus on the next month and year: what are the priorities? What is the sequence of activities? Who will do what? How and when will we measure performance? How will we remove obstacles to performance? Smithy has been at every high-level meeting since this thing started, and John, Bill, and Rory have been keeping him in the loop on anything he may have missed.

"The floor is yours, Smithy," I say.

"Thank you, James, and please let me thank all of you for your support so far. This has been the biggest project in my life so far and I am completely jazzed! I'll see it through from project creation to project completion and the ultimate handover of each output to the key business stakeholders. I will lead each project follow-up session myself, and when you tell me it's OK I will begin introducing my team to manage the many subprojects that will spawn from the main project. Each of the subprojects will of course have its primary focus on the overall project goal and I will take responsibility for the follow-up on those also. All of our progress will be wrapped up into a written biweekly exception report to highlight any shortfalls and the actions taken or required; I don't expect there to be many of those!"

"Monthly we will conduct a two-hour project update for the senior executives where we go over the complete status; no one will be in the dark, and in the interim short interval reporting will ensure nothing is allowed to wander too far off track for too long!"

"Smithy, who is bullying you into shaping your behavior and applying constant pressure on all of us?" asks John good-naturedly staring at Rory.

"I guess I'm learning a lot from all of you," says Smithy staying away from any finger pointing regardless of how good-natured it might be. "There is no question that I've learned the need for short interval reporting where immediate variances and problems pop up, and also where there can be longer term misses to our performance that might remain hidden and grow over time; our intent is to be on top of everything."

"Good answer," says John laughing.

"So I will begin with the high-level elements into which our current project will fit, recognizing that the subprojects will have to be plugged in later. The elements are as follows:"

- Project statement, which is an all-encompassing view of the three main features of the project charter. It becomes our reference point of what we intend to achieve by the end of the project, the timeline to achieve it, and any costs associated with this achievement. It is expressed in a written charter, which is agreed by the project sponsor, who, in this case, is the CEO. It is then displayed on the sides of a triangle for our reference and to remind us that any changes to the element on one side of the triangle will likely affect the other two.

  For example, it we increase the scope of the project it will likely cost more and take more time and if we reduce the budget for the project, it will increase the timeline for completion and likely compromise the quantity or quality of the deliverable. It follows that if we decrease the timeline available for project completion, it will likely cost us more or compromise the deliverable.

  It may be that more than one of these elements will be changed over the five-year duration of the project, but we must remember that this change will come with its consequences that in turn will affect many of the project elements and the outcomes that follow.

Project deliverable

Project statement triangle.

- Next we have the project objectives; these are the major outcomes we wish to achieve shown in a manner that makes them more actionable. They are shown in a bullet pointed list, which need not be shown in any priority order at this time. Given that the project objectives represent smaller parts of the project statement, the successful completion of the project objectives should equal the successful completion of the project statement, and therefore the overall project. When we do a back check to verify this and if we find their combined completion will not achieve this end, then it tells us there is something missing and we must find it. This process of doing a backward check or back pass of each major project element will help us ensure we are not missing anything all the way through the planning stage.

   In the development of these particular project objectives, we must consider the actions and outcomes we expect from the internal improvements we need to make in our four divisions. Also, any acquisitions we intend to make and their subsequent integration and the achievement of any planned synergies from those acquisitions. Other major elements that will be reflected in the objectives are communications, the embedding of any required cultural changes, the critical issues that have been raised for resolution in our corporate strategy, any critical issues that have arisen from our gated approach to our business growth, and of course the achievement of our financial objectives.

- Next we have the work breakdown structure (WBS), which further breaks down the work we must complete to ensure the meeting of all our project objectives and the overall project completion. It's back to how do you eat an elephant? One bite at a time! The bite-size pieces must be digestible.

   We achieve this by looking at each individual objective and breaking it into bite-size chunks. Over the years, I've seen different definitions of how big a bite-size chunk should be and they all have their merits. In truth, it should only be broken down to a size which is helpful for project completion. This is not a make work project so use your common sense and intuition as well as the inputs of others.

   When developing the WBS, there is no need for sequencing the individual activities; that comes later when we look for precedence relationships. However, don't be surprised if your elements fall onto the paper partially sequenced, your mind wants to be orderly so don't discourage it! We number the major element, subelements, and terminal elements of a WBS in a specific manner for consistency, and a simplified example would be

1.0 Move the office
    1.1 Determine new destination
    1.2 Create floor plan at new destination
    1.3 Organize move
    1.4 Conduct move

Each of the subelements could be a terminal element in its own right or broken down further. The terminal element is where the actual work is completed; again, an example could be

1.1 Determine new destination
    1.11 Review alternative destinations
    1.12 Select best alternative
    1.13 Secure lease

Again, it can be as complex as you need it to be, but don't make it any more so; it is there to serve you not you it, so keep it as simple as you can.

At the close of the development of your WBS, you will have reviewed all of your objectives and broken them down into actionable chunks; it's time for the back check yet again. Ensure that the completion of the terminal elements of your WBS will successfully achieve your project objectives; if this is not the case then once again we have missed something.

- Next we have precedence relationships. In looking at each terminal element of the plan we determine if some must precede others so that each can actually be started in turn. On the completion of this step, we can plot each element onto a Gantt chart so that we can determine the start date and a projected end date for each element. The duration of the time from start date to end date must be our best estimate and be based on lapsed time to completion; this is not necessarily the same as actual time applied for task completion. An example of this could be the painting of a house; although it might consist of 16 hours' work, the painter may only be available 4 hours per day, and so the lapsed time will be four days not sixteen hours.

  The Gantt chart has the benefit of not only showing precedence relationships and the lapsed time of each element but also the amount of work load that may be going on at any one time. It is therefore possible to move work load around to a later start date even if it has no precedence so that it might better space out available resources over time. There must, however, be great caution used here as some elements and tasks are on what we call the critical path. This means that if the task is delayed the entire project is delayed; there is no slack in the timeline of an element that is on the critical path.

Date/week Task	Week 1	Week 2	Week 3	Week 4	Week 5	Week 6	Week 7	Week 8	Week 9	Week 10	Week 11	Week 12
1.0 Move the office												
1.1 Determine new local	←→											
1.2 Create new floor plans		←→										
1.3 Organize move				←→								
1.4 Conduct move						←→						

Gantt chart example.

- Next we have responsibility assignment, only one person should have the primary responsibility for a tasks completion. It should not be a department. This eliminates confusion and ensures a go to person for status updates.
- Next we have resource requirements, where specific resources are necessary for the completion of a task they must be noted against that task. There tends to be different people who might require the same resource at the same time. Knowing this in advance can save future conflict by allowing for compromise. This could be as simple as the availability of a training room or as complex as a bank loan!
- Finally there is the monitoring and control that I talked about earlier. Each major project should be reported on for status every two weeks; the project managers will schedule and conduct these meetings with the relevant project stakeholders.

Each WBS element has a quantitative and qualitative deliverable; ensuring there is no shortfall or potential shortfall in these is the primary purpose of the status update meetings. They are also an opportunity to apply additional resources in case of a potential shortfall or alternately to accept that shortfall!

21

Communication and Final Broker Selection

I'm pacing up and down again; it seems I do this a lot. Am I just thinking or am I uneasy?

"John, come round will you?"

"What's going on, James?"

John actually seems to have rushed into my office; we both look surprised and laugh out loud.

"I guess I'm jumpy, John; why do you suppose that is?"

"Oh I don't know, billion-dollar decisions maybe," quips John, "I'm twitching a little myself old friend."

"How do you feel Rory is doing out in the field?" I ask.

"He's fine, making progress in his usual fashion of full speed ahead. Are you worried about him?"

"No...absolutely not, if I'm worried at all, it's about everything. Are we keeping up with the field from an M&A perspective?"

"I think so," says John, "but tell me what's next."

"Two things: our communication strategy and rollout and then our selection of the right broker to help us with the acquisition."

I call for Diane to come in, "Diane, can you set up two meetings for me? The first for tomorrow; get Helen from corporate communications in to see me first thing in the morning, say 8:00 a.m., for a premeeting, and then John, Billy, Smithy, Linda, and Rory to join us at 9.30 a.m."

"What do I tell them it's about?" asks Diane.

"The current and upcoming major project," I say. "They'll understand."

Diane turns to leave and I realize I've only asked for half of what I need. "Oops...sorry Diane, can you organize a series of meeting for Wednesday, same group from an inside perspective, but with one of the folks on this list of broker candidates for an hour each with thirty minutes in between. Also please ask all three of the brokers to be prepared to stay longer, maybe all day." I hand her the three names I got from Alex. "Oh, Diane, can you please get Alex on the line for me if he's available."

Tuesday morning at 8:00 a.m. and Helen is right here in my office; she seems a little flustered and that's not my favorite look in a communications officer. "Are you OK, Helen?" I ask.

"I am, James, to what do I owe the pleasure this morning?" she says looking around nervously.

"Take a seat, Helen," I say standing up.

"I think I'd rather stand, James."

"Helen what's going on here?" now I'm nervous.

"Well, I assume you're replacing me!"

"No…please sit down, Helen. What makes you think that?"

"Well there's been a lot going on, a lot of coming and going and closed door meetings; everyone is nervous. I'm more than a little bit embarrassed to have to admit that I am."

"I'm really sorry, Helen, not only for making you uncomfortable but for everyone else who has felt this way. Here's what's going on." And I explain the whole thing. "So you see it has had to be a controlled release of information and I clearly didn't involve you soon enough. I'm sorry Helen, it's been an oversight on my part."

"Now I understand," says Helen. "We'll need a good communications strategy starting today; it can still be controlled and based on what you've told me. It should be a good news story that can be timed in tranches to ensure we satisfy all of the stakeholders."

Helen and I discuss this for a while and then we are joined by John, Bill, Rory, and Smithy for the rest of the meeting.

"Guys…we should have been progressing the communications sooner!" Helen chides all of us. "You're all bright guys and must have known the dangers associated with rumors. Nature hates a vacuum, and in lieu of what's really going on, people make things up."

We are all shamefaced as Helen continues; she moves to the flip chart and captures our input for the communications strategy.

- The market place should not know we are planning an acquisition until further down the road.
- There should be no surprises for the board of directors.

- We need to inform the shareholders when our decision to go ahead is final.
- Our employees in the divisions should be informed of our intent to optimize the current business, they should also know our plans are growth based and that they should improve job security, not threaten it.
- There should be ongoing companywide updates of our progress to our employees, bankers, shareholders, and board of directors.

We discuss timing, content, and mode of communication and finally, Helen feels she has enough info.

"OK folks," she says, smiling at last, "I'll put a draft together for all of the elements of the plan including timing and get together again with you by the day after tomorrow for a review; we have to get this out there as soon as possible." And with that, she is gone!

Wednesday morning, we are moving along now. The team is in the office by 8:00 a.m., including Alex. The three candidates will be arriving for interviews at 9:00 a.m. We have decided to interview them in parallel with three teams, one team conducting each interview, Alex and I, John and Rory, and finally Bill and Linda. Each team will assess their current candidate against the stated criteria for approximately one hour and then move to the next candidate. We will then break off for lunch for an hour during which time we will review our findings on each candidate among our three teams.

Following lunch, all six of us will interview each candidate as a team, in sequence, to get a final team impression.

We decide to weigh each characteristic in relationship to each other with the most important being weighed a 10 and the others weighed in relation to this. The final list looks as follows:

- Track record of acquisitions in the $250 million range   10
- Knowledge of our targeted industries   8
- Superior people skills   9
- 15 years' experience as acquisition intermediary   5
- Suitable references   10
- Fee schedule in line with the industry   9
- Paid only if they introduce final company acquired   10
- Cutoff period 2 years to present each final acquisition   8

How well any candidate meets each criterion will be measured on a scale of 1 to 10.

The process proves to be a thorough one and our discussions as a team after our final meetings point to what seems to be a clear winner, Jane Austin! We all have a bit of a chuckle because of the irony in her name.

"Well, she should certainly be able to help us write a clear prospectus." quips Alex, ever the dry wit.

"I think she's brilliant," says Bill. "She ticks all the boxes!"

We all agree and arrive at a unanimous decision round the table.

"She is certainly very personable, got on well with all of us, and was thoughtful and responsive whenever challenged," I say.

"Not to mention the price!" says Bill. "Her overall fee will come in at about half a percent of our total acquisition cost, and she will bill us at a reasonable consulting day rate for any work she does on any partnering deal."

Linda jumps in, "I actually like the fact that she's a woman and that she owns her own company. I feel that her softer approach with prospective sellers will bring that personal touch and hand holding that owners of family businesses seem to like; they will trust her."

"She's fair," says Rory, "but no pushover. She held out for two and a half years before a cutoff if she has a hot prospect on the front burner, and I particularly liked the trust she showed in us when we told her that although we expected to acquire businesses to the tune of $1 billion in sales over the next five years, some of them might be small and privately held and others could be asset buys, even the possibility of a partnership arrangement. She very well knows that any of these circumstances could increase her workload and reduce the selling price to us and therefore her commission, but she stuck to her guns and to an overall half a percent!"

Alex seems to be enjoying the teams banter and how we think in general, and yet he brings us back to reality with a snap. "No one has talked about her experience yet. Are we sure she knows how to go about finding the specific targets we are interested in?"

I keep quiet, and John picks this question up, "Well, she certainly responded well to my questions regarding our current industries and our sector targets for expansion."

"Mine too," said Rory. "She seems to have more experience in the BPO sector of late, but her ten years in the field with one of the big houses before starting her own firm has given her broad experience with manufacturing and transportation companies."

Alex is satisfied, "So...we all like her; references in this game are critical, and so if they stand up, we have our person!"

"I'll have our head of HR check her references myself tomorrow, Alex. I'll even sit in on the calls and if they check out we will have her back in and go over our exact requirements with her by Monday. By the way, she has given you as one of her references. Is this OK with you?"

"It certainly is. She assisted me in doubling the size of one of my companies when she was with Smith and Smith."

22

Due Diligence...Don't Fall in Love Too Soon

I'm off to Europe! The teams are all set and working like beavers optimizing our company, it's funny how people get committed to a cause if they feel it worthy of them and this team clearly does, and so I'm off to Germany to conduct the due diligence on a possible carve-out.

I've traveled all over the world for business and pleasure, and yet I've never enjoyed the actual travel bit. People look at me and see me as a veteran, because I can fall asleep on a plane before it gets off the ground, they don't realize it's simply a coping mechanism, the truth is I don't like traveling, and surprise-surprise I'm also an introvert who has to blend in with an extroverted world; people seldom see us as we really are.

It's strange, when I was younger and poorer, the clients who I worked for flew me business class on all flights over two hours long; it was simply the policy. Now I am older, in higher level positions, and thank god personally wealthier than I was back in the day and now they fly me economy or premium economy. It's the new policy reality and it certainly doesn't make things any easier for the traveler.

I cope with the stress of travel by chunking it all down into little bits and I only focus on one bit at a time!

1. Get to the airport.
2. Check in.
3. Get through security.
4. Find my gate.
5. Get on the plane.
6. Get off the plane.
7. Get through immigration.

8. Get to the hotel.
9. Sleep.
10. Get to the office.

I do the same on the way home; it helps me stay sane. One of my best buddies calls travel brain damage, and he does all he can to minimize the brain cells he loses to it every year.

The purpose of this trip is to complete a due diligence on a business opportunity for our BPO business. We do a lot of technical and customer support for various clients, particularly in automotive and so this one is right in our sweet spot. When we purchased the BPO division two years ago, it brought with it a small European presence and so our companies only toehold in Europe. This opportunity promises us real growth; we have the automotive know-how. The company is interested in us doing a carve-out of a large section of their call handling and back-office business processing and then conducting it on their behalf. It is most definitely interesting for a host of reasons, not least of all the expansion of our currently small European presence and the cache of performing a soup to nuts solution for an important client in any industry, which can then be replicated in other companies and industries. It's also a large chunk of revenue and so the sales team is pushing it, as indeed they should be.

There's a general belief that outsourcers should be able to perform a function more cheaply than the company that is currently performing the work, and this is often true. But the question is, how much more cheaply? Every company is in business to make a profit and so normal pricing tends to be something along the lines of the cost plus model: the vendor determines their total costs and marks them up by the expected profit margin percentage. In the era of skinny profits, this does not leave much room for error.

It's natural that any potential new client wants it all and that includes higher quality than they are themselves currently achieving, and for a lower price to boot! Our sales guys have crunched the numbers and believe we can do the job for 40% less than the costs currently incurred by the client and the due diligence is to determine whether or not this is possible.

When I arrive at my hotel, there is a message waiting for me from the regional vice president of our business. I've never met him but it's a welcome message; it's an invite to dinner. I have time for a quick shower and just make it to meet him in the lobby; not knowing who is who in the zoo makes for a lot of awkward glances in any lobby.

"Rory? Hi, I'm Sam and this is Ellie, our VP of sales. How was your flight?"

"Hi, Sam, pleased to meet you," I say doing the normal shaking of hands. "Hi, Ellie, nice to meet you. The flight was fine thanks."

"There's not too much open for dinner on Sunday night in this town," says Sam. "But there's a little steak house across the square; we can try that if that's OK?"

"Sounds good, thanks, Sam." As we walk across the square, Sam explains that he is responsible for four call centers in his region and that Ellie manages sales across Europe. They want this one to work. There hasn't been a big project sold into our European business for more than a year. When we are seated and the food is ordered, the two folks get right into telling me what I'm going to find during the due diligence. They do a high-level introduction to the potential client company's senior management and the size of the business. They tell me I will have three guys working with me who have been on the project since its inception and another guy to help us translate documents, as none of us speaks German.

About twenty minutes into the discussion, I ask what I believe to be a couple of rather obvious questions: "What percentage earnings before interest and taxes will this piece of business yield our company and what is the total annual revenue for the project?"

To my surprise, I get silence and then blustering, "We have day jobs too you know; how do you expect us to remember everything?"

I'm amazed by the outburst of temper. After a pause, the VP of sales speaks up, "The project hasn't been priced in the traditional way; we simply said we would do it for 40% less than they are currently doing it. Don't worry though, it's not going to be difficult; there is plenty of fat built into the pricing."

I'm a long way from feeling reassured, "There must have been some kind of logic behind our believing we can do it for 40% less than they are currently doing it themselves," I say.

Ellie is calm and unruffled, while Sam looks like he's about to explode, so Ellie continues.

"They are very inefficient, long call handling times and very little coaching. Also we can save a bundle by off-shoring the non-call handling work to India."

"There was another major outsourcer who bid on the work before we did, but they dropped out and this gave us a second chance to win the business. They had previously offered to do the job for a higher cost reduction than 40%, and so if we wanted the business, we had to offer them a substantial reduction on their current costs to even be considered."

I want to support these folks. I know James and John would like to grow the European business and this would be a great jump-start for the new targeted overall company growth too, but the doubt in my face and the stiffness in my manner are telegraphing my thoughts to Sam and Ellie. I've arrived with almost no information on this one. John has left it in the hands of the regional guys, but clearly he is also uncertain. He told me to do a thorough job and to make sure we don't go over the edge of a cliff. However, he does not want me to make it impossible for him to say yes to the deal either!

I've packed for two weeks, but have been given no guidelines other than the speculation that two weeks ought to do it.

"So what's next, guys?" I ask.

23

Due Diligence 2...What Was That Again?

"Mind if I sit here, Rory?" asks Sam.

"No, not at all, mate; a good breakfast here, isn't it?"

"It's really the best thing about this hotel as far as I'm concerned, but that's good enough for me."

"Me too, Sam. Did you sleep well?"

"Yes...but I'm not really looking forward to the day; it'll be busy with lots of need to explain our approach to things and show everyone how nice we are."

"I'll be relying on you and Ellie, buddy," I say. "I don't know any of the players or where you are in the scheme of things."

"From the client's perspective it's a done deal already; both companies would like it that way. We want this business and so we have to win them over. It's like a beauty competition."

Ellie joins us, "Good morning, gentlemen," she says, sitting down and buttering a roll.

"Good morning," we both respond. Sam's direct look into Ellie's eyes shows a shared agenda.

"So the client thinks this is a done deal, Ellie?" I ask.

"Yes," says Ellie. "The company needs the sale; we are way behind our top-line target, so this has to happen."

"Then why the due diligence?" I ask. "Couldn't we just go straight to the contract negotiations?"

After a brief silence, Ellie responds, "We are already in contract negotiations; we meet face to face with the client weekly to hammer out the details."

"I don't see how that's possible before the close of the due diligence," I say, "and I absolutely don't approve of it."

Its Sam's turn and he raises his voice, "You don't know anything about this opportunity, you're not even an employee of the company, and you waltz in here telling us how to proceed on day one! Last night you badger us about the details of the deal and today you tell us we shouldn't be negotiating the contract with the client. You are pissing me off!" The outburst leaves Sam red in the face and he throws his fork down on the plate, gets up, and leaves the restaurant.

"This is a bad start," I say.

"Yes," says Ellie finishing her coffee. "I'll see you downstairs at the taxi in half an hour."

I have completely lost my appetite.

The cab has four of us squished up together and everyone is quiet. "So Ellie, what's the ideal outcome from today's meetings from your perspective?"

It's clear Ellie would rather not talk with me at all, she's staring into space, "We answer all of the client's questions and allay all fears that the client's staff may have about coming over to work directly for an outsourcer. We have to ensure them that their jobs will be secure with us and that they will keep their present salary and conditions, and that there will be no layoffs due to efficiency gains during the first six months."

"How can we promise that?" I ask.

"It's part of the negotiations so far and so it's contractual!" Ellie responds.

"I just don't get it," I say. "Surely nothing is contractual until we have reached an agreement and the contract is signed."

"Patrick will be here later this morning; he'll give you a view from the senior management perspective on why this deal is so important," says Ellie as she resumes her study of the glass that makes up the taxi cab's window.

Patrick is an old acquaintance of mine and the senior executive for the business in Europe. One of the benefits of bouncing all over the world is you get to know lots of different people. It is very apparent to me that I am being fed info one bite at a time.

The venue for the meeting with the client is in a local hotel. Several small conference rooms have been taken and the intent is that we will have four parallel meetings with all levels of client management present at each, everyone from vice presidents to team leaders. I discover that there will be eight of our people present today with two of us at each meeting.

I have been assigned to the same team as Sam and he is all sweetness and light with the clients' folks. The questions come fast and furious covering everything from job security to working at home, from salary to paid time off and vacations. Even the location of any new call center is suggested; we seem to be promising our lives away with just enough participation from me to show that I am not just an empty suit.

After a morning full of meetings, we leave in taxis and go back to our company headquarters to debrief and determine next steps. I am still at a complete loss as to the current status quo. The eight people from our company who attended today's client meetings are me, Sam, Ellie, two human resources people, one IT guy, a team manager from our local call center, and yet another vice president of sales. On debriefing the day's meetings, we find that all of them turned out to be pretty much the same and that our real goal was to present ourselves as the best possible partner and employer for the business, after all someone might just come along and offer a better deal!

Patrick breezes in, he's just flown in from London and everyone is falling over themselves because of his rank as senior vice president. He shakes my hand and gives me a manly hug; we go way back.

"Don't worry about this deal, Rory; it's a good one. We've built in lots of fat to ensure a minimum of 10% operating profit that should make the guys at head office happy."

"Who signed off on the numbers, Patrick?"

"Both European and corporate finance."

"Is the CFO in the loop?" I ask. "I spoke with him just before leaving the States and he had nothing to offer on this one."

"His department OK'd the numbers, so he should be up to speed," said Patrick.

We are all sitting around some tables that have been pulled together and we are joined by two folks who will be working with me on the due diligence: one is the project manager who put the schedule together and the other is an ops guy who created the spread sheets that show timelines, activities, and cost reductions, which are designed to show that the project can in fact be done for 40% less than it currently costs the client company.

"Where's the 10% operating profit?" I ask.

"It's baked into the numbers," says Patrick.

"Can you show me where?" I ask.

"It's been included as an overall markup of 10% to each line of the operating costs," says Ellie.

"I'll need to see it broken out," I say.

Sam blows up again, "Who do you think you are? The team has done a lot of work on this and all you bring is criticism. So far no one can see you as part of this team. Are you?"

I move to the flip chart and draw four quadrants titled total sales, profit, activity timeline, and scale of cost reductions and confidence level that it can be done.

Projected sales	Projected EBIT
Workload and timelines to achieve results	Risks and difficulties in achieving results

Profit analysis quadrants.

"We need to know that all four quadrants are in balance. Please tell me they are," I say to the room.

There is dead silence until Patrick finally says, "I think that's enough for the day; let's go back to the hotel and get cleaned up before dinner."

Patrick takes me to one side back at the hotel and talks with me over a beer.

"Rory mate, we really need this business and I asked James for you specifically to do the due diligence; I need your help here. Among other things, a new automotive client in Europe really hits our sweet spot."

"You know I'll always help you, Patrick. I want to help you, we go way back, but you have to show me that this won't hurt the company on the bottom line."

"It won't, mate. There's a lot of fat built into the profit line; we left a full two percentage points above our usual pricing in case there are any slip ups."

"Patrick, I'm hoping John or James talked with you about the changes in expectation in the company's bottom line; what we used to achieve simply won't do going forward."

"Yes, I got the memo! But this deal was in the works before any of the changes in expectation were announced; surely there has to be some kind of grandfathering on projects that are already underway?"

I pause, I'm thinking on my feet, but I know I have James' support.

"Agreed, buddy."

I pull out my notebook and scratch a few bullet points down for discussion.

"If the deal is strategic and can be grown or leveraged off later, we will go ahead at the currently planned margins, as long as these criteria are met."

- We can leverage off success and carve out additional parts of the client's business.
- The top-line revenue is sufficient to justify a current state margin of 8%.
- Our ability to carve out all of the customer contact and communications support areas with this client can be leveraged with future carve-outs with other clients.

"Are you OK with that, mate?" I ask Patrick.

"Yes, for sure," Patrick agrees.

"I'll position it with James, buddy, but I still have to perform the due diligence. I need to know that all of the assumptions that have been made so far will stand up."

"OK, Rory. Is there anything else that is concerning you at this point?"

"A bunch of things, buddy. I think Sam's behavior is a problem; he doesn't know any of the details of this deal, even the basics like projected EBIT and he blusters his way out of the questions. He tries to intimidate me, and if he is as aggressive as he is acting, what makes you think he won't react the same way with the client?"

"Leave Sam to me; I admit he is a little difficult. James has expressed some concerns to me about him in the past; did he mention him specifically to you?"

"No, I'm just telling you what I've seen so far. I'll leave him to you."

Patrick is making notes, "What else, mate?" he asks.

"Two things. I can't understand the reverse engineering of the pricing, so I have to know the 10% operating profit you believe is there will actually be there."

"OK, and what's the other one?"

"The spread sheet that shows how we arrived at the necessary improvements and how they relate to the financials; although all the numbers add up, it looks simply like a reverse engineering job to make it all fit together."

"You don't think we should do that, Rory?"

"It's all right as an exercise to explore the art of the possible, but it doesn't work without verifying the numbers actually work. Every line on the spreadsheet should be scrutinized to ensure the assumptions hold good, and how each assumption and outcome links with the others should also receive the same scrutiny."

"I think you'll find that it's OK," says Patrick.

"I hope so, buddy, but right now it's just numbers. There's no words, no explanations, no sign of the logic and yet everyone is treating this as if it's a done deal."

"They want the deal, mate! The company needs the deal!"

"If the deal holds water, then we want the deal, Patrick. I'll do everything in my power to make it go forward, but only if it is good for the company."

"All right, anything else?" Patrick asks.

"I don't understand the logic of ongoing contractual negotiations before the due diligence is complete!"

"It's to help us expedite the start date, Rory; we want to see the revenue in our fourth quarter results."

"I don't agree with it, Patrick; it creates expectations with everyone before the due diligence is completed."

"OK, mate, but I want to go ahead with contractual clauses anyway as it is widely understood that everything is contingent on the due diligence; we simply won't discuss financials."

"It's your call, Patrick, but I still don't agree."

"Let's have dinner and give you a chance to get to know the rest of the team," Says Patrick, and we shake hands.

24

Due Diligence 3…Look Before You Leap

We arrive at the client location for the first day of the due diligence. There are five of us, a director of human resources, the project manager, a senior operations analyst, and a young team leader who is along as general help, but more importantly for any needed document translation. We expect to be on site conducting the actual analysis for two weeks with a further one week finalizing our report at our local corporate office.

We are introduced to Heinz, the client's director seconded to us to help with the flow of the analysis, and then to all of the client's senior management team, some of whom we met at yesterday's information meetings and all of whom we will spend time with during the next two weeks. If the deal goes ahead, most of them are intended to stay with the new business entity.

We have been given a good-sized office to work from and the guys set up their laptops and get right onto them. How did we ever manage before computers?

"Hey, guys," I break the silence in the room, "I'd like us to get together for half an hour at the end of each day to review progress and ensure that we are all in the loop and singing from the same song book."

I get nods of agreement and yet I feel as if I am completely alone in the room.

The project manager begins talking to the senior analyst about the workload for the rest of the day; these guys know each other, they are buddies, and they are a team. If I try to muscle them into doing what I want, any help I get will be entirely passive, and so I have to influence them over time if I want their commitment and creativity. I don't like the approach of people's noses being buried in their computers and others, mainly me, being excluded, and yet that's what we have, and so for now I have to go along while still directing, very difficult really.

The project schedule has us interviewing the managers of the various groups, customer service, technical assistance, etc. It then has us sitting in the groups doing observations and collating our thoughts. Finally, there are mountains of documents in foreign languages to be worked through to glean which information is important to us; this work is delegated by the project manager to the junior manager who is on board mainly as translator.

Compounding the overall level of difficulty is the belief of the project leader and analyst as to why we are here, they know I'm the senior guy on the analysis and that I have a degree of authority, but they believe their own chain of command to be in charge and are really working to realize the objectives of those folks. They are being called and influenced every day by no less than four senior people from within the European organization. I am being tolerated and marginalized as a consultant who will move on, and if I kick too hard, they can possibly sink me!

During our regular due diligence working day, the senior analyst and project manager are also working on new proposals unrelated to the due diligence at hand, reading the contract to date and offering expected changes to the responsible sales VP, joining and even leading conference calls on program launches and other ongoing projects, and delegating work not associated to the current due diligence to the junior manager.

I go along with the flow reluctantly and so we gradually gather baseline information on the running of the business, and the sales guys continue to negotiate the contract with the client. At the end of each working day, everyone is still busy and overloaded, working into late evening.

Two days into this, I am extremely unhappy, and so we have the first impromptu team meeting right in the middle of the day.

"I'm unhappy guys; I don't know what's going on and even what you are working on! Why do you have to be doing all of the work on other projects during the due diligence on this one?"

Neil answers, "We have no choice, I'm the only project manager in Europe and everything can't just stop because of this assignment. Terry is the senior analyst who creates all the models and spreadsheets for new business and there is an additional model due for this Wednesday for another sales opportunity, so what is he supposed to do?"

I say, "I will talk to your senior VP and the COO and have them assign additional resources to Europe until this due diligence is done."

They don't like that and come up with a dozen reasons why that won't work; they say everything will be fine.

"We can get all of the work done between ourselves," says Neil. "It just means we will have to pull a few all-nighters, but we're used to that."

"I need to know where we are each day," I say, "or we might run out of time and out of opportunity! We will have to catch impromptu times to talk about project status and direction during the working day"

Terry and Neil exchange glances "OK, but we'll have to call our bosses to let them know what's going on," says Terry.

"That's fine, but in the meantime, I need clarity on a few high-level points!" I say, walking to the white board that stretches along an entire wall of the office, which has been completely unused up to this point and I begin to write while talking.

Things we need to know

- What is the actual transition and ongoing workload that must be carried out each month of the project over the coming five years?
- How much of the current work being done onshore will be offshored?
- How many jobs will be terminated onshore?
- What will be the cost burden to our company each month?
- How will we manage the transition?
- What will be our recruitment requirements both on- and offshore?
- What is the expected attrition level from the client company estimated at?
- What danger is there of not meeting existing client contact volumes and service level due to potential disruption during the changeover?
- What impact will there be on customer satisfaction levels during and after the transition?
- Will there be any deterioration in the client's market share?
- What potential costs will our company face due to penalties for missed targets?
- Has the client already achieved the targets they will be holding us responsible for achieving?
- What corporate and management resources will our company allocate to this opportunity?
- How do we intend to achieve the 40% cost reduction target? Through reduced call handling time? Technology? Reduced labor costs? Offshore labor arbitrage?
- What is our company's breakeven point each month?

- What is our expected EBIT performance each month? Each year?
- Is the expected 40% cost reduction phased in or from a standing start?
- Is there a massive day-one change required to achieve the 40% cost reduction and is it possible and sustainable?
- Are there any unknown costs that our pricing model has not considered?
- How much low-hanging fruit/potential cost reductions is there?

It's reasonable to say that after we go over and digest the bullet points on the white board, we stop to ponder, "So what do you want to do next?" the project manager asks.

"It's not so much what I want to do next," I say, "it's what *we* want to do next that's important; I thought all of us were part of this team and I still do. If we are one team, then we are responsible for one outcome, and if that outcome is negative, we all lose. Am I missing something in this logic?"

"We have bosses," says Terry. "We were asked to develop a spreadsheet to determine what had to be done to meet the 40% cost down expectations, and that's what we have shown you."

The projector clicks on again and the spreadsheet is flashed up on the wall.

"Where is the risk analysis associated with it," I ask, "and where are the words? I don't see any words! Do you guys simply communicate with numbers? Are numbers less risky, more difficult to pin down to an individual? It's taken me two days to get this demanding, shame on me!"

"If you need words to understand this, then you will find them in the project plan," Neil responds defensively.

"So let's go over the project plan," I say. "I've already read everything you sent me by e-mail prior to my arrival, but I may have missed something."

We go over the plan line by line and balance the activities against the Gantt chart projection of the timelines. It's all very high level and lists all of the departments that we will analyze and the individuals we will interview.

"What is our expected outcome from each of these activities?" I ask.

"To see where we can find the savings," Neil replies.

"That would amount to removing four out of ten people from each category, and that's without any cost being attached to making the changes," I reply. "Do we really think that's possible?"

"That's what sales have committed to," says Terry. "It's in our letter of offer; it's a done deal. There's nothing we can do to change it now!"

"Nothing is a done deal until the due diligence is done and the conclusion is a clear go ahead! At that time we will sign a contract, and right now, I feel we are a long way from being able to commit to that!" I say. "Who suggested that a 40% reduction was possible and what was the logic?"

"Sales came up with the number," says Neil, "and if you want to know the logic, you should ask Patrick. Anyway, the company needs this deal to grow the European business and to hit this year's numbers. It's already been passed by the COO and he agrees with it."

"Well unless I've misunderstood my mandate and I don't think I have, the reason I've been sent here by the COO and the CEO is to ensure these numbers make sense and that it's not one big elephant trap that our company is going to fall into. That's my most direct way of telling you that while I am here I represent the COO. How do you explain this letter you e-mailed me?"

I hand over an unsigned one-page communication to the COO that is pushing for acceptance of this deal. Neil scans it and then reads it more carefully, he then hands it to Terry who does the same.

"I would have missed this!" says Neil to Terry, who simply shrugs in response.

"It clearly states that we expect to reduce the overall current client costs by 25%; that's what the COO has given his provisional agreement to. You have gone through your spreadsheet with me twice now and I must admit to finding it hard to follow, but I do understand that the total reduction it shows comes to 36%. How did we ever get to 40%? Which number is right, 25%, 36%, or 40%?! Are any of them right? Has finance been working on these numbers? Have they been agreed by the CFO?"

There is very little reaction in the room other than the body language equivalent of foot shuffling. "You would have to ask Patrick the answer to that," says Neil sheepishly. "You can't blame sales for pushing the deal; that's their job, right?"

"Not at the expense of taking the company down a blind alley," I respond.

"What are you going to do?" asks Neil.

"We, remember, we are going to do two things. I am going to write a letter to Patrick asking which of the three projected cost reductions is the real one and ask who in finance validated it. I will remind him that the extent of the reduction in cost to the client must be reflected in the activities we conduct to achieve it, and the bigger the number, the tougher the project. I'll show you the e-mail before I send it."

"And what about everything else we are here to do?" asks Neil.

"We do it! It will take a few approaches in parallel that should validate each other. We sit with each of the groups you have identified and look for cost savings, we look at organization charts to see if there are threats or opportunities in the span of control and if there are opportunities to combine groups to create synergies, and we ask questions at all levels of the organization to answer the questions on the white board," I say, pointing at the bullet-pointed list.

25

Due Diligence 4

The due diligence is a bit of a grind and really so it should be. If you want to find out if the acquisition is viable, you have to be on the premises for about two weeks. Sure you can tell yourself that you have all the data and that you can study it in the comfort of your own conference room and that e-mails and telephones are there for asking questions. I'm afraid that's not going to do! There simply is no substitute for eyeballing the prospective acquisition or the client and seeing the operation; you never know where the key tipping point information will come from.

One week in, we get a call from John, our corporate COO.

"How's it going, Rory?"

"Hi, John, it's bumpy. The client wants an update every few days to check on our progress; his real agenda is to determine if we have found anything that would stop us from going ahead."

"And have you?"

"Yes, potentially there are lots of things; I think we are a long way from being able to say this deal is going forward."

"Have you told the client that?"

"Not directly, I take the position that we have a further weeks due diligence to go before we will know, which is a true and accurate position. Our project manager tells him that we are exactly where we would expect to be in the process, and although that's true from a task perspective, we are still a long way from knowing if we should go ahead with this."

"Are you getting pressure from any of our guys to make it work, or for that matter to walk away from it?"

"Just the usual, John. The senior sales guys have a vested interest in going ahead, as does the local regional VP; I understand that. I've also been getting a bit of a push from the VP of facilities to rule on it now, she thinks it's a no go and so a waste of time and money and she wants to know what my gut tells me before the analysis is even over."

"Yes, she called me. What did you tell her, Rory?"

"Initially nothing other than we didn't know, but she wouldn't let go, so I told her I didn't believe it would go ahead at 40% less than the client was doing it for. I told her that the analysis could give us a platform to negotiate down to around 25%, but even that only if it held strategic value for our company.

It's a bit of a piss off that sales are still negotiating clauses for the contract with the client when we simply don't know if we will be able to go forward. Do you have any words of wisdom for me?"

"A couple of things would help me at this end, Rory. Could you push our sales guys to let them know we will have to negotiate price? Get them ready for it."

"I can, and I can also tell the senior on-site guy for the client that there will likely have to be some negotiating done."

"Good, but don't make it impossible for us to say yes to the deal at this point; leave us some wiggle room."

"Will do, John."

We continue the due diligence as planned on two fronts, individual analysis of each business subgroup and targeted high-level questions. During the in-depth subgroup analysis, we work in two teams with two of us in each team. We spend around three hours in a conference room environment with each group asking and listening to achieve understanding of the functions undertaken by each group. We then spend time out on the floor doing side-by-side analysis with two agents minimum in each group, with as many as six side by sides for the larger groups. The groups we analyze include

- Customer assistance
- Technical assistance
- Project management
- Parts
- Engineering

In all cases the team managers know that there will be a need for cost down within their teams, they suggest the easy cost reductions like not replacing people who are on long-term absence or the combining of groups that will result in the elimination of duplicate functions and the saving of a couple of folks. What they do not know is that an overall 40% reduction is targeted and that this would mean an across-the-board reduction of four people in every ten across all functions. The cost downs they offer hardly scrape the surface of this, but we listen, probe, and learn.

The interviews with senior managers across the business reveal a lot, and as always we dig deeper when we can smell a lead.

In addition to analyzing the data we are given, we ask for key data in certain formats, an example being key performance indicators plotted over the last twelve months to show actual performance against targeted performance. This has disclosed that the targets we are expected to achieve within the first sixty days of taking over the business have in fact never been achieved before, or achieved only sporadically. There are substantial penalties associated with performance and although this is acceptable, it is only acceptable if the targets are possible and within our control; if we cannot achieve them, we will lose what razor thin margin we have.

We also spend time going over the spreadsheet that we have developed to support the needed activity levels and cost reduction targets associated with achieving the 40% cost down expectations.

At the close of the two week due diligence, we clarify the following:

- There is zero ramp-up time allowed to hit the 40% cost down expectation, it must be achieved day one and continue throughout the five years of the contract. Any delay in day one achievement is rolled forward and increases the ongoing target.
- We cannot change salaries or staffing levels within the first six months.
- Our pricing was intended to be based on 30% of the work being off-shored, resulting in a gain from labor arbitrage; it has however been based on 60% of the work being offshored.
- The work designated to be offshored is non-customer facing, off-phone work, but this has not been segregated into specific work-groups and the non-phone work is in fact used to fill in the time between incoming calls allowing for maximum agent utilization. It also includes time to research information to resolve problems in real time.
- There is an opportunity to automate some of the back-office non-phone work.
- Customer facing phone work must remain in the host country.

- Assumptions on call average handle time reduction are extreme, up to 25%.
- No coaches have been priced into the project and they will be necessary to achieve the projected reduced average handle time.
- A great deal of low-hanging-fruit opportunities have been realized by the client in the last twelve months; 150 people have been released.
- The company subsidizes meals and coffee for all employees; this amount was unknown until now and is substantial.

On relooking at the numbers, we find that a total of 10% reduction in the client's current operating costs is the most we can offer, but we know this will not be enough to have the client go ahead with the deal. The senior vice president of sales believes that the client will accept an offer of a 25% reduction from current operating costs. Coincidentally or not, we have heard this same number confidentially as being a likely deal breaker from a client manager.

On our conference call with John and Billy at head office, we go over the five-page report we had sent them earlier, once again, on the recommendation of local senior management. It's really just a series of numbers starting with the original client costs of operating the business; we then add any previously unknown client costs we discovered during the analysis and also any additions we have made to our costs due to needs found during the analysis. When it is all tallied up at the bottom of the page, the analysis showed that we could offer the client 10% reduction on their operating costs.

John and Billy pushed sales on why they had ever assumed we could reduce the costs by 40%, and sales indicated it was an aggressive estimate to keep us in the game.

We discussed the strategic benefits to our company in running a complete carved-out business of this size in the automotive sector in Europe and they were considerable, and so I suggested that I would lead the integration and commit to finding an additional 10% bringing our offer to the client up to a 20% reduction on their current operating costs. John asked me if I was sure that we could pull it off and I said yes, but with an understanding that the risks were high and that any unexpected costs would eat into our planned 8% EBIT. If, however, the strategic benefits outweighed the certainty of the bottom-line performance, we would commit to the 20%, but no more.

When negotiations resumed with the client, they refused the offer as they believed that they could get a 25% cost reduction on their own.

26

The Communications Strategy

Helen is as good as her word. Two days after our initial meeting, she is sitting in my office with the senior team to give us a preliminary view of her proposed approach as to how we should communicate our company's intended growth; everyone is here except Rory, as he is still in Europe.

"How are you, Helen?" I ask, hoping she has forgiven me.

"I'm good, James, thank you. Hello everyone."

"Hello, Helen," the mob choruses back.

"I suppose you are wondering why I have invited you all here today," she says chuckling at the spirit of the group's hello.

"Yes, Helen," we all chirp.

"Enough! Stop!" she says, and we are silent.

"It's nice to see everyone relaxed and it's nice to feel relaxed myself," says Helen. "This is how people react when they are in the know; however, a lot of our people are not in the know and you can bet the grapevine is not silent."

"Sorry, Helen, I've admitted my tardiness to you in how I have handled communications so far, and with your help, I'd love to put an end to the workings of the grapevine."

"I don't mean to go on about it, James, let's move on. You might be a little surprised about how I propose we proceed though!"

"And how is that, Helen?"

"Tell everyone everything right away," she responds.

We all fall silent for about thirty seconds, "Well that sounds a bit sudden, don't you think, Helen?" I ask.

"James!" she says, "Everything that you are proposing and doing is positive: you don't want to take away anyone's job, you intend to grow the core business and are already taking steps in that direction, and you have done acquisitions before albeit a lot smaller than you have in mind now.

I know we have to plan our communications carefully and we will most certainly do that, but it strikes me that it's time to get at it...now! You should be proud of what you are planning to do; it's a good thing for everyone."

"Thank you, Helen," I'm genuinely moved. "How do you feel we should progress?"

"Strangely, it's relatively simple from a planning perspective; there are two main initiatives, although there are multiple audiences. First we have the organic business improvement and growth initiative, and second we have future potential acquisitions."

"It strikes me that the first item is largely internal and positive and that you already have it under way. I think we should communicate it within the next two weeks to our major stakeholders; the sequence could look like this," and she moves to the flip chart and writes as she speaks.

- Brief the board of directors on the overall communications plan with a copy of the proposed communication for shareholder distribution and the proposed method and timelines for company-wide communications, explaining that any questions should to be directed to the corporate communications officer.
- Distribute communications to shareholders; also distribute relevant press releases.
- Bring the senior division executives and management in for a briefing and make full disclosure to the senior execs on all growth plans.
- Make full disclosure on their being a potential for acquisitions.
- Leave the senior team with an understanding of the mission (internal top-line growth of 33% with a growth on the profit line of 50%, and further top-line growth by acquisition over the next five years while maintaining the new improved EBIT).
- Create the message for employees with same basic information always focusing on the positive aspect of business growth.
- Determine the size of the groups to be briefed across the entire business (20–60 people per group).
- Determine who will lead the briefing groups as facilitators; they must not be cynics and must be positive-minded individuals.
- Train the facilitators in presentation and communications skills.
- Create a frequently asked questions and answers sheets for distribution (Q&A).
- Schedule fifteen-minute briefing groups across the company.

- Ensure any external questions are directed to me (corporate communications officer).
- Conduct communications to the employee base over a twenty-four-hour period max.
- Follow up the face-to-face communications with biweekly update memos.

"Regarding the second element of the future acquisitions

- Include this in biweekly updates with any high-level relevant information as it arises.
- Ensure SEC rules around timing are complied with regarding any information release.
- Ensure truthful and appropriate communications companywide as legislation and good sense allows regarding all progress (from corporate communications officer only).
- Ensure board of directors and company senior executives receive all biweekly corporate updates prior to general release.
- Ensure progress on corporate goals is communicated biweekly to all employees."

"This looks good, Helen," I say. "What are your thoughts around communications when an actual acquisition is in process at one level or another?"

"Well, based on what you have told me so far James, it seems that there are no real targets in our line of site at this time. It also looks like you might do four or five acquisitions in the $200,000,000 range and that triggers certain assumptions on my part."

"And what would those be, Helen?" asks John.

"That all of them should be on board and contributing by the close of year five, and that this will imply the likelihood of a staggered or sequenced program beginning relatively soon, say one per year in a perfect world?"

We are all nodding in agreement.

I say, "There is a general consensus of thought out there Helen that it can take a full year to find and close an acquisition, do you think that this implies we will have nothing to report on the acquisition front for twelve months?"

"Too long a period with no comment after suggesting that this will likely be part of our long-term plan would lead us back to speculation through the grapevine," Helen responds. "I think we should make comment in our bi-weekly coms from time to time about our ongoing search; they should be circumspect but honest."

"And when we finally make an acquisition, Helen, what then?"

"We will launch a series of communications across our existing business and to the employees of our newly acquired business, as well as to all of our customers and suppliers in both businesses. This of course will cause a considerable flurry everywhere, including the press, and will take a lot of our time and attention, but handled properly, the excitement will calm down and edge back into normality. It won't be dropped though, not ever. Rather, it will be folded into our existing communication and receive ongoing love and attention, and then we will do it all over again with the next one."

"Can you give us an idea of what this set of communications should look like, Helen?" I ask.

"I'll have to sit down with human resources and operations to create an entire program around this, James. It's something we will use again and again with added improvements over the coming five years and maybe beyond, but for now, I'll go over a few initial thoughts."

And with that Helen moves back to the flip charts and writes from a stream of consciousness as she speaks.

- The right integration leader is crucial; that person will set the atmosphere and future results for the entire initiative.
- We must have a clear expectation of which management will be retained in the acquired company, and whether or not their current leader will be their future leader.
- The integration leader should either be the new leader of the acquired business for a period of time or work as an equal partner with the existing leader or his replacement until the integration is complete.
- The lines of authority of management at all levels must be clearly communicated to all stakeholders, including customers and suppliers.
- On day one of the acquisition, the senior executives of both companies should be active in announcing the merger or acquisition to all of the employees of both companies.
- All senior executives up to and including both the CEO of our company and the CEO of the acquired company should be present and visible on the floor, with both of the CEOs physically present on the ground at the newly acquired company on day one.
- Both companies' human resource departments should be present side by side where possible during communications.

- The message should be honest and reflect the growth plan of the combined companies.
- All ongoing communications should reflect the mission of both organizations and the benefits that the merger offers (increased market share, improved customer service, etc.)
- There should be high visibility and high levels of management by walking about in the weeks and months following the acquisition.
- Face-to-face communications are always best; we have to make the time.
- In-depth information packages on the acquiring company should be made available to the acquired company with a questions and answer sheet as to how the merger will affect the new employees (benefits, etc.)

"There will be a heavy burden on all of us from a time perspective from now on by the looks of it Helen; it feels a bit overpowering, as if we will have to be in many places at the same time. Is that even possible?"

"It's what we have to do, James; sometimes we forget the importance of communication because of our workloads. These are the times that we are communicating anyway, usually by default! Our body language, our focus on issues rather than people, which has us walk past them in the hallway as if they are not there. They say good morning and we walk right past without even seeing them, the end result of an unconscious moment like this by us leaves the person feeling snubbed and wondering what they did wrong; it can stay with them for months, and they'll tell others! All of us do this to some extent from time to time; think of how much bigger the need for communications when something is really going on!"

"I'm with you Helen. I hate it when I think I have inadvertently disrespected someone; it lingers with me too. What tools do we have that will allow us to communicate better, in many different places at the same time if necessary?"

"Thankfully there are lots," says Helen moving back to the flip chart and writing while she speaks.

- Face to face is always best.
- Video conferencing is good, but limited to meeting-room-size groups.
- An actual produced video from the CEO or other senior executives can be viewed many times by different groups.

- The biweekly newsletter updates.
- E-mails.
- The good old memo.
- Every possible method of communication should be used!

"What else do you have to tell us today, Helen?" I ask.

"Sorry James, I know I am taking up a lot of everyone's time! I'll bullet point the rest of the salient points for today and then we can talk about follow-up!"

- Consistency is required; every communication should be anchored to our overriding goal of 33% growth and 50% profit improvement. This is a growth story that benefits everyone.
- Ensure we have mechanisms in place that encourage feedback.
- Training must be supplied at all levels for those who will conduct the group presentations.
- There must always be consideration as to whom/which people hear a communication first.
- Our messages should be structured to fit our specific audience, always truthful and relevant.
- Poor communications will result in poor follow-up.
- Never stop communicating. This is a process not a project; it goes on forever. Remember the grapevine will take over where we leave off!

"I'll stop here for now, James; I think I am leading everyone into information overload."

"Thanks, Helen, any questions from the group?"

Linda raises her hand, "What are the next steps, Helen?"

"I'll get these notes cleaned up and typed for James to run past the chairman of the board for agreement. If this is received I'm sure James will distribute them to the group."

"What else, Helen?" asks Bill.

"I'll create a communications matrix and schedule to determine who does what and when. After James has made any modifications he may have and agreed the content and timing, we can get going, the sooner the better; next week would be good."

I thank Helen and the team gives her a long round of applause.

Helen smiles her appreciation. "Sorry for being such a bitch," she says.

"We love you Helen; thank god you're here!"

27

Rory McGregor

It's been six months since John walked into my office on that fateful Saturday morning and found me staring out of the window, me deep in thought and him thinking I had the best job in the world.

"James, it's just as well you didn't stare out of that window earlier, or you would have nothing to do right now!"

I love John; we've worked together again and again, and for so long. We've helped each other through thick and thin; he simply seemed to understand and accept my epiphany about the need to grow the company without question.

It's funny how we live our lives meeting hundreds, no thousands, of good people and working very closely with them to achieve chosen goals, and yet we seem to have only a few close friends. John is such a friend; I'll always work with him, probably until the day one of us dies. It seems like guys like us never retire!

Then there's Rory, another old friend, more like a brother really, him and John both; in fact, we used to call ourselves the band of brothers. I find that I'm musing a lot these days thinking of the past and the future, as if the present wasn't full with enough surprises, both good and bad.

It's time I talked with Alex, he has to be kept up to date on our progress, and so we'll have dinner tonight.

I meet with Alex in Beppi's; we've booked the small private room in the rear of the restaurant again. Beppi has allowed us to book it for the full night and he is waiting the table himself, a real honor for us!

"So tell me, James, how is everything working out so far? Do you believe you are on schedule? Are there any insurmountable obstacles in our way yet? Are you meeting all your gated targets?"

I laugh out loud and so does Alex, "You know, it's bad form to ask any more than one question at a time Alex and there you are banging out four in a row! It's good to see you old friend; even if you ask me all these questions you already know the answers to before saying hello!"

"Good evening, James," Alex says still laughing as he stretches out his hand.

"Good evening, Alex," I reply shaking the hand of an old friend.

"I'll go over this without taking all night and potentially disturbing a great meal, Alex, and then you can tell me what would be appropriate to share with the board at this stage."

I commence the high-level overview, "As you know, we have selected our mergers and acquisitions broker and have her undivided attention until we find the right acquisitions for us. We have clearly defined the type of companies we are targeting, all privately held or divisions of larger companies that don't quite fit with their current owners and plans, without exception they are all chosen to plug into our current businesses synergistically. So far we have been presented several possibilities, all of which we have vetted to determine if they will fit our needs and are in line with our strategy. There are enough of them that passed the test and remain on the table ready for us to do preliminary site visits. All of them look like good possibilities, but we are very much aware that we may have to look at a lot more companies before finding the right ones. John and Billy along with a couple of handpicked guys will go out to each of these over the next couple of weeks to determine if we should look more deeply under the covers. In the meantime, our agent continues to beat the bushes for other possibilities. So I would answer your question about being on target and meeting the gates we set ourselves with a resounding yes."

"What about the internal optimization of our existing business?" Alex asks.

"Also on target," I answer. "The profit performance of all four divisions has gone up by an average of a full 2% already. Rory says that it's really due to the Hawthorne effect, you know, give it lots of focus and attention and it shall improve. He's shortchanging himself though; he knows what he's doing."

"And what exactly is he doing, James?"

"He's involving the management and employees all across the company and giving them the tools to find opportunities; he's actually teaching them how to analyze their own business. On top of that he's treating them as equals and listening to what they have to say, he's helping them pick the low-hanging fruit and making sure that they get all the credit for it. He's also setting up management control systems that ensure we are monitoring and acting on the right things, and solving problems when they come up, not simply firefighting recurring problems."

"Do our guys know how to do that?"

"He's teaching them, Alex, he has picked a small group of champions, disciples might be a better word. He has trained them as trainers in all of the necessary skills and they in turn are teaching the rest of our employees; it's largely learning on the job and so the business continues to run uninterrupted."

"Good God," says Alex, "that sounds like a huge job for any one man to pull off. Are you telling me it's really possible?"

"It is if you're Rory McGregor," I answer. "But it's not just one man, sure Rory is the nucleus but the trick is getting everyone behind the wheel as quickly as possible, and then pushing it up the hill."

"Are you saying that Rory is creating supermen who in turn are creating miracles?"

"Maybe I am, but they are everyday supermen creating everyday miracles, they want to please him."

"Why?"

"Everyone wants to be a part of something big and to be respected for their part in it. Rory goes at his work from the belief that everyone wants to do a good job, he gives them direction, impetus and recognition, and on top of that he is one of the last true charismatics! Most of them love him and want to be like him; they know they will be stronger for the experience."

"You say most of them love him; what about those who don't?"

"There aren't too many people who are middle of the road with Rory; people tend to either love him or hate him. He demands lots from himself and the same from everyone else, from the janitor to the CEO, no exceptions. He told me once that the greatest compliment he can be paid is for someone, anyone who does a good job, to treat him as an equal and offer him respect for the job he is doing. He puts himself above no one and simply wants the good forklift driver to recognize that he, Rory, is doing a good job too."

"You've known Rory forever, James and it's clear you respect him greatly. I know you pick your friends carefully, so tell me a bit about how you came to know him, and who is he really?"

"Well, he didn't have the best start in life, by his own reckoning pretty hopeless in school, unteachable really. He was born in Scotland, his father a shipbuilder and his mother a welder. The father left when Rory was eleven years old, so it was a tough life. He knew that he had to get a trade to save himself from a life of being an unskilled laborer, and so at sixteen years of age he did. Highly typical of the man he would become he found a mentor who taught him math, something the Scottish school system had failed to do, but something he needed to get the apprenticeship in the mechanical trades!"

"That's very commendable, James, but how did he become so skilled in management processes?"

"He would tell you that it was simply a natural progression over time, but a lot of time. He got his first real foreman's job at thirty, but before that he finished his apprenticeship as a millwright, sailed as an engineer on oil tankers, worked as a tool and die maker in the automotive industry, and worked as a charge hand and senior rig technician in research and development."

"What drove him?"

"He had to feed his family and he believed he wasn't that great at anything he did, so he worked harder than most anyone else, and he just kept going."

"Tell me about his management and consulting career," said Alex, full of interest.

"He worked as a production foreman in an automotive machine shop, then as a shift manager in high-speed packaging, then on to training and development and running the continuous improvement program. He moved into consulting with one of the big houses and eventually formed his own consulting company. Over the years, he has fashioned himself as half-consultant, half-executive and has turned around divisions of four automotive companies, several metals distribution companies, a pharmaceutical business, a food company, a division of a major electronics business, and more than one outsourced call center business. As an executive he has held positions ranging from general manager through president, COO, and managing director in metals distribution, plastics, and BPO contact centers. He has led businesses all over the world always successfully."

"I'm impressed," says Alex, "but it all begs a big question, why hasn't he been working for you at our company until now? John and you have been largely inseparable during your careers, but not Rory, why?"

"Easy answer," I say. "He retired about five years ago and has spent his time traveling the world. I offered him the job of managing director running our European business around that time, but he said no."

"So he's financially independent?"

"Yes he is, Alex; by most people's standards you might actually say he's rich."

"And yet he's here, working side by side with you now. Why would he do that if he said no to you earlier?"

"Because I told him I needed him; it's simply loyalty."

"That simple?" said Alex.

"That simple," I echoed. "You probably wouldn't recall him specifically, but he came back around three years ago and closed down our business in Africa, no small challenge as he had to liaise with the government and jump through lots of fiery hoops to do it. He didn't want to do that one either but I really needed him to. Our senior guy on the ground was leaving the business in a matter of weeks and I needed a good guy on the ground."

"I remember that," said Alex. "We hadn't hedged the pound against the rand and the rand had strengthened, and as all of our costs were in the rand, the business became unprofitable, right?"

"Right, but he actually turned it around during the five months he was there and he did everything in his power to bring on a new client, his job was to close the business, but he tried to save it!"

"This guy is taking on mythical status right before my eyes, James."

"There's more. The emotional aspect of turning around the business and then still having to close it down, I'm afraid that one nearly broke him. The word is he was in tears over it way more than once; he couldn't stand the prospect of losing seven hundred jobs in Africa so he moved heaven and earth to try to save it. He never quit."

"Is he OK now?"

"He says he is, and he seems to be, but there's no question that one really did a number on him."

"He told me that he had been preaching the need to support the three main stakeholders in business equally for years, the shareholders, the customers, and the employees, you know, the three-legged-stool story. But he said he hadn't really understood it, felt it, until Africa."

"Well, he is certainly contributing to making this one interesting James!"

"Yes he is, Alex, and he will most certainly succeed; he never considers failure to be an option."

"You left one little part out of the African story James; my memory tells me that the client paid us one hundred thousand pounds in bonuses after the project ended."

They did. Rory kept his management team in the loop on everything and they supported him to the last day achieving all the hard measures set by the client, including customer satisfaction. Rory and I made sure we paid the employees double the amount we were legally responsible for in redundancies, he trusted them and they trusted him and so they took care of the client and our shareholders, and we took care of them as best we could.

"Alex, can you come over soon and spend a day with the executive team?"

"I can, James, but why a whole day?"

"I'd like the senior team to be involved in giving you a full update on where we are so far and where we believe we are going."

"I can do that," said Alex. "Anything else?"

"Yes, I'd like you to be present while we workshop our corporate culture. It's important that any acquisition we make fits in with the culture and lately I've been worrying a bit about ours."

"How so?" asks Alex.

"Well, I guess I always believed that the CEO set the cultural direction of the company by belief, actions, and example. I've walked around with the absolute belief that if I had an open-door policy then all my execs would, and if I managed by walking about, then my team would, and if I thought fairness in all of our dealings was the only way, then the team would too! You know all that stuff."

"And your beliefs have been shaken, James?"

"Yes, most definitely! I feel as if I've been living in cloud cuckoo land! I feel that if the success of our objectives is largely to find acquisitions that fit with our culture, we should know ourselves as a good well-run company made up of people who care, and to do that we might have to reinvent ourselves before we integrate anyone else with us."

Alex nods pensively, "Look at your team's calendars and set up the day, James; give me at least a week's notice if you can."

28

Status Update to the Chairman
of the Board

We have expanded our circle regarding the knowledge of our overall plans and today our entire executive team is present when Alex arrives at 9 a.m. Sitting around the conference room table are the four divisional presidents: Billy, the CFO; Linda, the VP of sales; Smithy, the director of projects; Helen, our communications officer; Joyce, the VP of Information Technology; Valerie, our VP of Human Relations; John, the COO; and Rory. All of them rise respectfully as I show Alex into the room. Although all of the folks have met him at one time or another, few of them are really familiar with him as a person. Consequently there's a lot of handshaking and reintroductions around the table.

When we are seated I open the discussion, "Well, now that we are all comfortable with each other again, it's my pleasure to open the floor and have us jointly walk Alex through our plans, intentions, and results to date. Before that, I'd like to ask Alex to say a few words."

"Thank you, James," says Alex. "It seems like a long time since James first approached me about the potential opportunity of significantly growing our company. I can't say that it had never crossed my mind, but I can say that I had never been bold enough to float the possibility with James, so his approach to me was timely and surprising. The primary role of the board of directors is to ensure that the shareholders' interests are protected, our role is not to run the company, that's management's role. As you are aware, there must be a degree of overlap in these roles or the board would not have enough information to make informed decisions on behalf of the shareholders and so James, your CEO, has a place on the board in addition to his role as senior executive of the company. Over the time I have known

James, he has kept me informed both formally and informally regarding what is going on in the company and this has led to an informed board, trusting relationships, and mutual respect, all of which are critical for good human relations. You can understand therefore that I was open to James's approach, albeit more than a little nervous. Since then you have all worked diligently and made significant contributions to the work conducted on the initiative so far. I thank you for that and I apologize for the periods of time when each of you might have been left in the dark prior to signing confidentiality agreements and being brought into the light. I'm talking my head off today and that was not the plan, so with these final words to convey to you that you have my complete support, I'm handing you back over to James."

"Thanks, Alex," I say. "Although you are largely up to speed on our progress and that none of this will come as a great surprise to you, we felt it was important to bring together all of the elements of our work to date and show them as the pieces of the puzzle that they are and how they interlink with each other. All of us will play a part in the presenting of the information and then be available to answer your questions. Finally, it was my hope that you would join us in workshopping what we believe our company culture should be going forward."

Alex nods and smiles. "I'll be pleased to," he says.

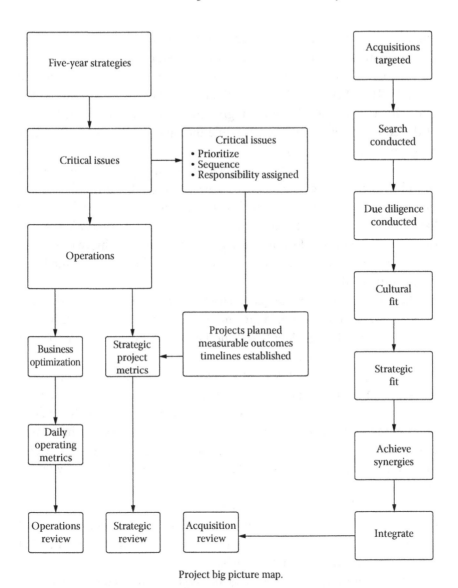

Project big picture map.

We now begin to move through the pieces of our presentation using pictorial overheads to support our presentations. I start with strategy highlighting the need for improvements in our internal business before considering acquisitions.

The division presidents pick up on this with their new mantra of 33% and 50%, 33% growth in top-line sales and 50% growth in profit. Alex asks each of them how they intend to achieve this and when and where they are in the process now. To which each in turn explains the timeline and quantifiable expectations. Each gives a high-level explanation of where they are now, and that is on target. They are confident and proud.

I then explain our synergistic approach to any acquisitions we intend to make. That they will add an additional $1 billion to the company's top line, which along with the internal growth will effectively double the size of the company within five years while maintaining our new 12% EBIT performance.

Linda goes over our current product market matrix and indicates our confidence in the areas of opportunities for growth, Billy talks to the financial implications, John and Valerie talk to the key capabilities we have and those we must acquire, and Smithy handles the critical issues that have to be resolved in the strategic time frame to achieve our goals. He also shows their sequencing and how they will each be handled as a series of interlinking projects.

I then move to the targeted acquisitions themselves and show the synergistic benefits they will bring to the overall business, maintaining and growing their existing client bases and becoming suppliers of goods and services to our existing divisions.

We all chip in to explain the benefits of having our own transportation company, an inhouse supply of cans through owning the production lines, the savings in overall materials costs through expanding the extent of our internal metals supplies to automotive and the can company, the benefit of expanding our food and beverage lines through the acquisition of a candy and soft drink business, and a generic pharmaceutical and vitamin company.

We also explain our intent to broaden our value add to our automotive customers through increasing the volume of subassemblies offered and partnering with an offshore auto parts supplier to increase our global reach and take advantage of labor arbitrage.

We talk of our intention to leverage our content knowledge as a supplier of technical assistance telephone support services and customer assistance services supplied by our BPO business to the automotive sector. We have been handling the escalated problem-solving support calls from the dealers' mechanics for years, as well as handling direct calls from the car manufacturer's customers for support. Our intent is to acquire an automotive marketing company to increase the breadth of product and service offerings available to our existing automotive clients and to leverage off of the acquired company's existing clients to sell our existing and highly acclaimed automotive services.

We also intend to acquire an offshore call center business in the Philippines, India, or Africa to take advantage of labor arbitrage and offer blended lower cost solutions from both on- and offshore locations, which will also improve our current disaster recovery plans.

During all of this, Alex is listening intently and following along with our overhead schematics.

"What do you think so far, Alex?" I ask.

"I think it's great," he says, "but I have a couple of questions."

"Please go ahead," I say.

"The first one is for you and Bill. How are you going to pay for all of this?"

We repeat in detail the methods we had introduced earlier, Bill taking the lead then me, then everyone joining in spontaneously. They all know the plan!

"Next is for Valerie. How will you ensure effective HR integration?"

Valerie goes through the entire due diligence checklist and explains the intent to partner the acquired companies HR teams with her own to ensure continuity of our new and expanded business beyond the merger; both teams will always work side by side.

The questions continue in this vein with Helen responding and detailing the communications plan and Joyce going over the IT plan.

"From an IT perspective, we don't expect any great degree of difficulty, it will not be necessary to bring all the new locations onto our existing platforms, we can continue to use their existing technology so long as it works well, and so long as we can ensure we have the necessary connectivity so that our expanded divisions can interact with each other. In that perspective, it will only be a partial integration."

Alex singles out Rory, "It's one thing to get everything firing on eight cylinders in the beginning, but what do we do to ensure it stays that way, Rory?"

"It's our intent, sir, to perform wellness audits on the business every six months, to ensure that the processes we have put in place are still relevant and working. We will refine them in real time and if necessary replace them."

Alex nods, "Won't that cost a lot of money?"

"You might have noted on the overhead, sir, that we intend to develop a small internal consulting company, largely made up with the folks we have trained so far to conduct the analysis and business improvement. They will only be deployed/borrowed from their day jobs as the workload requires and a nominal charge back will be made to the divisions, based always as a small percentage of the results achieved. It is also our intent to offer consulting to our clients and suppliers, we believe we already have valuable and desirable skills that go beyond the job content skills in the respective divisions. The intent is that this consulting company will operate as a profit center to the overall corporation and not a cost center."

Alex nods, "And who will run it?" he asks.

"The intent is that I will, sir," responds Rory.

"Good," says Alex.

"James, show me the mechanisms you have in place to reduce any probability of failure," asks Alex.

I go over the gated approach we developed earlier, except this time it is shown as a sequenced Gantt chart with milestones set showing the minimum targeted performance expectation to be achieved before advancing to the next step.

	Year 1				Year 2				Year 3				Year 4				Year 5			
	Q1	Q2	Q3	Q4	Q1	Q2	Q3	Q4	Q1	Q2	Q3	Q4	Q1	Q2	Q3	Q4	Q1	Q2	Q3	Q4
Metals division	Year End (Y/E)	Sales		EBIT	Y/E	Sales		EBIT	Y/E	Sales		EBIT	Y/E	Sales		EBIT	Y/E	Sales		EBIT
Automotive division	Y/E	Sales		EBIT	Y/E	Sales		EBIT	Y/E	Sales		EBIT	Y/E	Sales		EBIT	Y/E	Sales		EBIT
Food and beverage	Y/E	Sales		EBIT	Y/E	Sales		EBIT	Y/E	Sales		EBIT	Y/E	Sales		EBIT	Y/E	Sales		EBIT
BPO division	Y/E	Sales		EBIT	Y/E	Sales		EBIT	Y/E	Sales		EBIT	Y/E	Sales		EBIT	Y/E	Sales		EBIT
Acquire Auto Marketing					Y/E	Sales		EBIT	Y/E	Sales		EBIT	Y/E	Sales		EBIT	Y/E	Sales		EBIT
Acquire Contact Center					Y/E	Sales		EBIT	Y/E	Sales		EBIT	Y/E	Sales		EBIT	Y/E	Sales		EBIT
Acquire Chocolate Company					Y/E	Sales		EBIT	Y/E	Sales		EBIT	Y/E	Sales		EBIT	Y/E	Sales		EBIT
Acquire Pharmaceuticals									Y/E	Sales		EBIT	Y/E	Sales		EBIT	Y/E	Sales		EBIT
Acquire Transport Co.													Y/E	Sales		EBIT	Y/E	Sales		EBIT
Establish Auto Partnership													Y/E	Sales		EBIT	Y/E	Sales		EBIT
Establish Consulting Business													Y/E	Sales		EBIT	Y/E	Sales		EBIT

Project milestones/company growth plan.

"Finally," says Alex, "how much will it cost us to complete the overall M&A and internal improvement exercise?"

Bill answers the question, "To buy the additional businesses, we have identified it will cost less than one times sales, so less than $1 billion. I can say that because we are targeting only privately owned companies, asset purchases, and a joint partnership. The consulting business is a greenfield startup done by ourselves, and we fully expect and commit to all acquired businesses being accretive during their first twelve months of ownership."

I'm proud of him, Alex is proud of him, everyone is proud of him, and I'm proud of everyone!

"Are you OK with this, Alex?" I ask.

"I most certainly am James," says Alex. "And I want to thank you all very much"

He is smiling from ear to ear.

"OK all, let's grab a sandwich and spend some time this afternoon looking at our best selves, our culture!"

29

A High Performance Culture

I guess we always need a break, something to stop our minds racing for a little while. Years ago when I was a kid studying for an exam, I read something that suggested our mind was at its best for learning when it studied for twenty minutes or so and then stopped for five to ten minutes before getting back to studying, then keep repeating the study–rest process. It seems that the mind digests and consolidates the information learned from the study periods during the subsequent rest periods! This technique worked for me, but it might not be for everyone. Nowadays I find it a little hard to get going again after a break, such is life!

"Any words of wisdom to get us started, Alex?" I ask.

"Yes," says Alex, "the briefest of thoughts," and everyone laughs, including Alex.

"It is considered that one of the biggest causes of failures in Mergers and Acquisitions is a miss match between the cultures of the two companies involved. It is very difficult to change the culture in any organization let alone merge the cultures of two different organizations so that they can function in harmony with one another.

I've been impressed and then fascinated by the way your business has diligently gone about the task of optimizing your own performance prior to purchasing and integrating another. It may seem like a straightforward thing to do, but you'd be surprised how rare it is. It's been equally interesting I'm sure for each of you to discover that you all have differences in your beliefs and cultural norms that have come to light during this process."

Alex has a way of getting everyone on the edge of their seats and this is no exception.

"Once again I am delighted as to how you have decided to approach this as a team. Not to simply state that you know what your culture is and then seek out companies for acquisition that meet the final criteria of being a cultural fit with you. Instead, you have decided to review and if necessary recreate the culture that you want to have—one that is transportable in part or in full. I'm excited to see how all of this shakes out!"

With that, Alex hands the floor over to me. "Thank you, Alex," I'm up and at the flip chart in a heartbeat; I intend to facilitate this one myself. "Someone start me off with what they think the core/the apex of our culture should be," I say addressing the room.

Bill speaks up, "Like our strategy demands, high profit."

I write it down, "Anyone else?"

"People centric," says Jennifer from the BPO division.

"Accountability based," says Harry Wordsworth.

The entire spectrum covering people's views comes out and I capture them all on the flip chart.

"A culture of trust," says Valerie.

"Results driven," says Smithy.

The list continues to grow and I take all of them until we have filled a full flip chart page, conspicuously neither John nor Rory have spoken as yet. John looks directly at Rory and Rory nods to him.

"A high performance culture" says John.

I write this at the top of the next page. "Do we have one now?" I ask.

"No," says Dave Mason, "but I think we can all say with honesty that we are working toward being one."

"The list on the previous page is a good list," says Linda. "Every one of the team's ideas has a place in our culture; generally speaking they must have, but none of them completely captures the essence of what we must be going forward. I think a high performance culture will contain all of these ideas."

The room nods their agreement. "Are we ready to start building on what that means?" I ask.

There is a resounding yes, and so we begin brainstorming.

A HIGH PERFORMANCE CULTURE

We don't have one yet but are working toward it, we have the desire and wherewithal to build on and replace if necessary our current culture until it fits the model of a high performance culture.

CHARACTERISTICS

- Can be replicated
- High levels of accountability for performance
- Responsibility
- Respect
- Appropriate consequences for behavior and results
- A gain sharing plan for everyone
- Recognition
- Mutual support
- Trust
- Honesty
- Clear performance expectations
- Feedback mechanisms
- Short interval performance reporting
- An entrepreneurial mindset cross company
- Accessible leadership
- Knowledgeable leadership
- Know how sharing across the company
- 360° reviews to tell each of us how we are perceived
- A fair performance management system
- Suggestion box with a feedback mechanism that is actually used
- Fairness

The inputs to the list slow down and we decide to bring it to a close, with the proviso that HR will circulate it to all levels in the organization for feedback.

"All levels?" asks Tony Dent.

"All levels," replies Valerie.

I continue, "To make this workable and transportable, it will have to be incorporated into a working model, something that drives our behavior and performance, something with triggers that move us toward the desired behaviors and discourages those which are undesirable. It has to be a posted document with subelements right down to each operation and interaction to keep all of us on track. Valerie, will you head up a working group on this?"

"Gladly James," responds Valerie.

"I'd like to be on that team," I say.

"I'll canvass the leaders and the divisions to form a core team and the respective subteams at all levels," Says Valerie.

30

Spreading the Message...Train the Trainer Skills

"Good morning, co-conspirators."

"Good morning, Rory," they echo back, the handpicked team, the chosen men and women are all here.

"And how have you all managed without me when I was sunning myself in Europe," I ask.

"Oh it wasn't easy," says Roberta, "but somehow we've stumbled along; everything is on track."

"Thank you all, I'm nothing without you."

"Oh, we know that, Rory!" We're laughing, we're a team.

"I think I must have had too much time on the plane to think, which is always dangerous. It occurred to me that you will have to spread the good word and give more of our people the necessary skills to keep this puppy turned around, are you ready for that?"

"It's timely, Rory," says Tony, "people are asking for it. They see that we are growing and that the company is growing and they want to get on the train."

"OK my dear friends; let's start with the bones of how to pass on knowledge...not only a training program, but training our folks so that they know what we know and can do what we do, in this way we can continue to expand the circle."

These folks are brilliant; they are leaning forward, keen to learn new skills and keen to get to pass them on; they are indeed like sponges.

"Let me roll through the basics," I say, moving to the flip charts with my trusty pens.

"If you have the space always use four flip charts laid out next to each other just as you see them here. It gives you great flexibility for a host of reasons and beats out overhead projectors for training every time and for very good reasons."

- They are more intimate and interactive, the lights are on and everyone is home!
- You can show the equivalent of four different slides at the same time, much better for retention.
- You can capture the inputs from the group you are working with in real time, and post them on the wall.
- You can start with the big picture as bullet points and maintain them on the flip chart to your far left.
- You can then relate each step you flesh out on the remaining charts back to its sequence on the big picture chart on your left. This lets people know where they are in the process, also where they have been and where they are going.
- If you use break out groups, you can put one of your flip charts in each corner of the room for the groups to work out their assignments and ideas on.

The team is scribbling out there notes; some of them are photographing the charts with their cell phones. I wait a couple of minutes to let them catch up and gather their thoughts.

"OK?" I ask. They're quiet and some are still looking down but they are nodding, and so we continue.

"There's great power in working through new information from big picture to little picture. People tend to get lost trying to digest large blocks of new information and can benefit from the help we can give by chunking it down into bite-size pieces for them to digest.

"You focus on the main concept of the process you are teaching, and then go to the first substep, all on your left hand flip chart, and then you continue the breaking down and clarifying of each substep in turn on your remaining three flip charts."

I show the team as I proceed, developing each step on my flip charts.

- On flip chart two you define WHAT the sub step actually does for you.
- On flip chart three you explain WHY this works.
- On flip chart four you show HOW you do this.
- And also on the fourth flip chart you create an EXAMPLE of the whole."

As always, the team is jibing at me; it seems they can't let any opportunity go.

"Hum...so are you saying we really need five flip charts, Rory?"

"Is that a trick question?" I shoot back, as good naturedly as any Scot can pretend to be.

"The more flip charts the better I always say, but most often we scrabble to get four in the room and so we have to improvise. You know, taping stuff to the wall, writing on an available white board, adding something to a sheet we have already used, flipping a page, you get the picture. The main trick is to show a logical flow of the information you want to convey; keep it visible for your participants for as long as possible before moving on, and always relate it to the main teaching point and sub teaching points. Let people know where you are, where you've been, and where you're going."

"Will this work with any content, Rory?"

"Yes, you have to shape the content to fit the delivery process, but yes. The processes we will most often teach are thinking processes; remember these processes are a vehicle to gather and organize information and so they are really like your old mother's clotheshorse she used for drying her washing, they are simply a frame for hanging and organizing ideas and content."

God I love to see the wheels spinning behind people's eyes as they are digesting the value of a new idea and this team is like a good healthy field ready to accept the seeds I am offering them. I think it was Mark Twain who said:

> A human mind once stretched with a new idea can never return to its original shape.

"Let's look at some of the thinking skills," I say. "First, there is a difference between linear and lateral thinking skills. They both have their place and often fold over onto one another. The linear thinker tends to follow a logical series of steps to come to his conclusion, whereas the lateral thinker tends to follow a more spontaneous and creative approach often going off on tangents that get them to the desired result. Examples of processes we can use for lateral thinking would include brainstorming and story boarding where a facilitator captures the free flowing thoughts of a group and writes them on a flip chart or individual cards that are then stuck to the wall.

Rules are few and far between; it's the free flowing brains and minds of the group that create the outcome together. If there are rules, they would include a lack of judgment being passed on anyone's ideas and the piggybacking of one idea on another. Also stating the complete opposite of an idea is good; that's not criticizing!

Once these ideas have been generated and the flow of information from the group seems to have stopped, it is often a good idea to comb the list, eliminate duplicates, and combine similar ideas as long as it does not detract from either of the originals.

Finally, it is a simple matter to prioritize the list for further action, in the creative process this is usually best achieved by the vote of the group."

"Talk to us about some of the useful linear thinking processes, Rory."

"Well thank you, thank you, thank you; I was just about to mention that! You know I put a great deal of stock in processes and yet at the end of the day it's just thinking! I've spent so much of my life teaching and applying thinking processes that I benefit from them second nature, just like breathing. I have a wide array of processes in my toolbox and yet no firm favorites, it's simply a matter of selecting the best tool in your toolkit for the job you are currently doing. We've already used project management, strategy, four-point planning and managing the performance system. We applied the right tools to the right job."

"I'm going to go over a few others with you now," I say, moving toward my trusty flip charts.

- The Ishikawa or fishbone diagram is a great tool taken from Statistical Process Control and attributed to Dr. Ishikawa. A diagram of the skeleton of a fish is drawn with six major bones and a head. The problem to be solved or issue to be resolved is written in the box that represents the head. Each bone has one of six major headings written on it representing *man, measurement, material, method, machine,* and *environment.* The group or individual engaged in solving the problem write possible causes or contributing factors on secondary bones coming out of the main bones carrying the headings. This is continued until all ideas are exhausted. At this point it is legitimate for each member in the group to select the top five or so causes that seem most likely to them. The number of votes for each possible cause can be written against it on the fishbone diagram, this will not necessarily identify the most probable cause, but it will help narrow the field.

  The group can then discuss the overall findings and select the top one or two most likely causes, which can then be tested to verify whether or not it is the true cause. As always, the final test for true cause is implementing a fix, and if the problem goes away it looks like you got it.

However, you should always stay cognoscente to the fact that more than one possible cause when combined with each other can result in the true cause and the subsequent elimination of the problem.

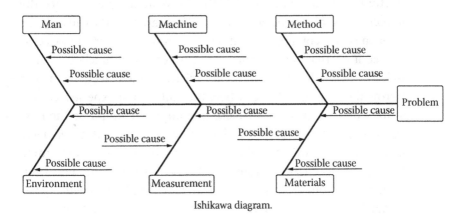

Ishikawa diagram.

- Situation analysis is a great tool to apply to multiple problems that together are creating complexity. First you list all of the component parts of the situation that you can think of, and making them visible makes it relatively easy to prioritize them against each other to determine the sequence for their resolution. Then it's a matter of assigning each prioritized component part or problem to the most likely suspect available to take primary responsibility for its resolution. It's also a good idea to assign a target date for its resolution and set follow-up meetings.
- Decision making is a tool that allows for the best possible alternative to be applied achieving an outcome if it is not clear which alternative is best from a number of possibilities. The trick is to know what you want to achieve and you do this by brainstorming the objectives that will be met by the best alternative and then testing each alternative against those objectives to find best fit.

  Remember that there is risk in any alternative and it's better you find it now rather than later. You can do this by asking what can go wrong if we go with a particular alternative; some risks you can prevent, some you can live with, and some you can't.
- Problem solving is only necessary if there is something that is going wrong and that you don't know the cause, or something that is not

performing to expectation. If you know the reason for the lack of performance you can simply fix it; if, however, you don't know the reason, you can apply the problem solving thinking process to find the cause or at least narrow the search. The process is the equivalent of taking a picture of the problem in four dimensions (1) WHAT exactly is the problem. (2) WHERE do we actually experience the problem; this most definitely narrows the search for the cause. If the problem is on a component that is being produced where do we actually see it on that component, any cause can most likely be traced back to where a force of some kind relates to the defect. To further narrow the search, a view of where the fault is first experienced in a production line, process, or piece of equipment would be the next logical step. (3) WHEN the problem first occurred will be valuable in leading us toward a possible cause as it will allow us to determine if anything has changed around that time, if the part has ever been produced without the fault it is logical to assume that something has changed. Also any pattern in when the fault appears will help us find the cause, if it is present on every part, we can likely see it happening in real time; if it happens at measured intervals, we can time those intervals to possible changes. If the problem comes and goes with no discernible pattern, it unfortunately makes it harder to find. (4) The EXTENT of the problem is a huge help in narrowing the search for cause; if there are four machines feeding a process and 25% of the components have the fault, it likely leads us to one of the machines; if it is 100% it leads us to something that touches everything in some way. A combination of these reference points on a picture of the problem will give us a test bed to compare possible causes against which to determine the most likely. As always, the final proof that we have found the actual cause of the defect is to fix it and see the problem actually go away.

"Now remember guys, processes help us through giving us the equivalent of a clotheshorse to hang our thinking on so that we can assess our thinking in an organized way. I firmly believe that any good process will do; the process is there to help us, but how have I asked you to view each process?"

"The process is there to help us not to drive us, at the end of the day it's all about thinking!"

I love these guys!

31

The M&A Shortlist

Our M&A broker has done a great job in the desk screening of potential opportunities on our behalf. When I try to tell her how wonderful she has been and how much we are impressed with her, she simply says that it's her job. I know for sure that none of us could have achieved what she has, and yet she says that she is just getting started!

The formal report to date is being delivered in our board room at head office, all of our usual suspects are present, and everyone is keenly interested, including Alex, who says he just happened to be in the neighborhood!

"So far I've desk screened a little over one hundred potential companies that could fit your needs," she says. "It is a bit of a grind, but at this stage it is largely a numbers game. Most of the really good companies are not for sale and even if they are they don't admit to it, and so my potential opportunity list comes from several places as opposed to just the obvious and the companies that are listed, who you know can be very important."

You could hear a pin drop in the room.

"I'm particularly grateful for the work your team has done in defining the targets; it has made it relatively easy to eliminate a great many prospects by just doing phone work, often needing no request for further information from the companies. I worked through listings from the SIC codes, contacted brokers who had business's for sale on their lists, got leads from old friends and acquaintances, and made some cold calls to company owners after securing an introduction to them from my contacts."

"A great many of the potentials were eliminated because of your specifications, which include

- Size of the organization targeted from $50 million to $400 million
- Privately held companies
- Pay one times sales maximum

- Possible interest in divisions of companies that don't fit the parent company's strategy
- Turnaround situations acceptable
- Asset purchases preferred
- Partnerships to be considered
- Purchases to be spread over the next three to four years with the first being sooner rather than later
- Some specific geography requirements"

"The strategic acquisitions map you provided and the brochure you put together about your company along with the desired characteristics of your potential acquisitions were very helpful. I currently have eight businesses identified for your further examination and probable site visits. I have had to compromise a little on your stated requirements, usually on the size of the business, but it is all transparent in the details I have supplied you on the prospects."

The broker pushes more than 12 pages across the table to me and Alex, each set neatly paper clipped with a triangular cardboard corner fastening them together in the top left-hand corner. She then hands out sets to each of the others at the table.

"Don't leave them lying around!" she chides with a smile.

"This three ring binder," which she holds up for view and then passes to me, "contains those that did not make the cut with the explanation why. Hold onto it for now as we might choose to revisit it later."

"We are all eagerly thumbing through the pages proffered moments ago; the stage still entirely belongs to our intermediary."

"My favorites are," she smiles

1. The high-speed packaging plant; it's older and has two can lines, drawn and ironed (D&I) as per your request. Maybe you could use one for food and one for beverage as per your wishes?
2. An empty call center with 500 seats in South Africa, which should meet your offshore requirements for the BPO business.
3. An automotive marketing company, which services most of the North American manufactures and some of the offshore ones. It's based in Michigan and should complement your core automotive capabilities.
4. A transportation company, which owns its own fleet but has lost some business of late and has underutilized capacity.

5. A generic pharmaceutical company, which is not meeting its productivity targets and struggling to integrate a line of vitamins, including omega-3 fatty acids capsules, which it recently acquired.
6. A partnership with an automotive stamping, welding, and assembly company in Mexico.
7. A partnership with an automotive assembly company in China.
8. A small boutique candy bar and chocolate manufacturer.

"That's it for now," she says. "I'm still looking!"

We are all dumbstruck, although Alex is smiling.

"I think it's brilliant," I exclaim, and everyone agrees enthusiastically. "What do you think the next steps should be?"

"Well, I think we should go over these one at a time and determine what we think each is worth; we can do that right here in the office, and I of course have my own thoughts on that. I believe you can have all of them for considerably less than the $1 billion you have planned for, this could leave you dry powder for a second wave after you digest the first."

"Why do you think we can do it so cost effectively?" I ask.

"I actually assumed from your overall directions coupled with the internal optimization work you are also doing that this was your desired outcome, you know minimize risk."

We all laugh. "Please explain my dear," says Alex breaking his silence.

"The can plant, the South African call center, and the transportation company can likely be done as asset purchases. The automotive marketing company is a strategic misfit division within a large services corporation and is losing money. The pharmaceutical company is in some trouble and needs your help; interestingly I find that its founder and CEO is an old friend of yours James! The two offshore automotive companies need cash, attention, and the leverage your current automotive business and metals business can give them. And the candy and chocolate business is delightful but has never grown to its potential; the owner will welcome the merger with your food business."

"I think I should meet with each of their owners personally," I say. "Just a cozy one-on-one lunch to determine what they think and want, and to tell them a bit about us. I will be careful not to fall in love too soon and avoid any negotiation at this point, but I think I want them to love us!"

Our intermediary agrees. "Good," she says. "After each of your meetings, assuming you are still interested that is, I would like to go in for a site visit with two or three hand-chosen executives of yours to each business. If I play the intermediary on these visits, it should help defuse any animosity that might arise through some of the things your team might find. It's too early to get tough, and we are still at the courting stage."

We are all happy with that.

"Each of you has your expertise; we should be taking a retrospective three-year, high-level look at the financials, the sales, and the customers; the serviceability and quality of the assets; any human resources implications and any legal implications. It is crucially important that we are always aware that there may be something badly wrong with the potential acquisition hiding just below the surface. Trust your intuition as well as the information you gather, but don't blow the deal. Remember this is a preliminary site visit and not the final due diligence; we hope it will always be love at first sight and yet we are still courting."

I thank Jane, our intermediary, and the rest of the team and close the meeting accepting Jane's offer for her to set up the lunches as soon as possible on my behalf.

32

What We Are Working with Is Time and Space...Synchronous

I can't really call these guys the analysis team anymore; they will of course continue to analyze and yet they are well into the business improvement stage. In truth, it would be most accurate to call them the continuous improvement team. We are all sitting round the table together in the corporate board room, John and me and sixteen heroes. James just popped in to say hi, drank a cup of coffee with us and as usual thanked the guys, shot the breeze, and left; it was as simple as that. John and I are just sitting among the folks talking about the weekend when Linda and Smithy pop in, completely uninvited.

"What are you two doing here?" I ask.

"We smelled the coffee," says Linda, and she and Smithy walk up to the table at the end of the room, pour their coffee, and snag two of the best smelling hot muffins. Then would you believe it, they each find an empty chair at the table and sit down among the team.

"Oh, excuse me," I say, "this is a private meeting."

"Sure it is, Rory," says Linda, "give with one hand and take away with the other. Didn't you say you have an open-door policy in all circumstances?"

"Oh...well, you might as well stay then," I shoot back, as if what I said would make any difference.

"Sorry, Rory," says Smithy, "we thought you wouldn't mind and we both hate to miss anything."

I wink at Smithy, making sure it's on Linda's blind side, "actually you are very timely as we are going to talk about sales, albeit indirectly."

It's all gotten very cozy with our little team, it looks like we've got trust working for us and according to the folks on this team we also have it in the divisions. I just continue to sit with the folks and chat. "Would anyone like to hear a story?"

"Oh…yes please, Rory," says Linda.

"Then we'll begin," I say. "Once upon a time, much longer ago than I would like to admit there was a big bad ogre who lived in the woods… actually he wasn't really an ogre, he just seemed like one at the time. Anyway, more than twenty-five years ago the automobile industry was in very bad shape and one of the industry leaders had a brilliant idea; they called the idea synchronous. I suppose it might have been a kind of fore-runner to Lean because its sole objective was to remove waste from busi-nesses and processes. They used it on themselves, gathering a trusty band of magicians much like you to weave the necessary magic, and it worked! Next they decided to send the magicians into the field to help their suppli-ers to also reduce waste; there was no charge for this but there was a stipu-lation that in future all business would be awarded to the lowest bidder. But…but…but…we have better quality than everyone else one or another supplier would proclaim. 'Good,' responded the magicians, because that's the price for entry; anyone without superior quality would not even be considered to bid for the business. And so everyone initiated synchro-nous; there really wasn't any choice, and it resulted in a lot of waste being removed from hundreds if not thousands of businesses and processes… and we all lived happily ever after!"

"Is that it?" asks Smithy, almost throwing down his pen.

"Are you kidding?" asks John. "He hasn't been talking for nearly long enough yet!"

"So you want more? Then I'll continue, the process had a definition for what constituted a value-added step and there were three criteria:

- The step/activity had to CHANGE the actual thing in question.
- The change to the thing had to be perceived as a VALUE ADD by the end user.
- The activity or change to the thing had to be done RIGHT THE FIRST TIME.

Process mapping was used at two levels, companywide and process spe-cific, to identify each step any product went through and to identify the time each of those steps took for completion. Next, each step in turn was assessed against the criteria to determine if it was value added or non-value added. The process mapping was conducted at the two levels in sequence:

1. At the life-cycle level from order to delivery. This map would show the various departments that the THING moved through to completion logging the time spent at each step in the process. It was total lapsed time that was logged. If, for example, a document took two minutes to process but was left waiting in a basket for two hours, then the lapsed time recorded would be two hours plus two minutes, not simply the process time of two minutes.
2. At the individual processes, the THING had to flow through in any given department; the same scrutiny was applied.

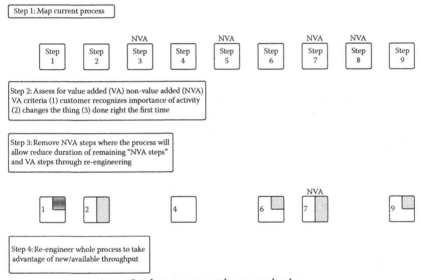

Synchronous map at the process level.

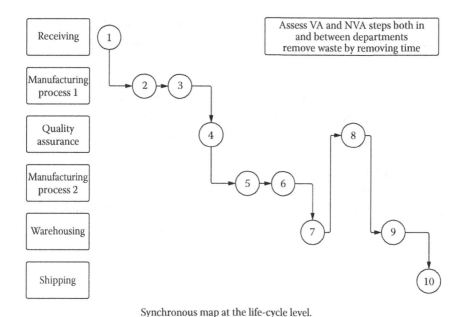

Synchronous map at the life-cycle level.

The next step was to simply remove any non-value-added steps, or if that were not possible, to reduce their duration as much as possible! It's amazing how few steps pass the three criteria established for value added.

The overall objective was to remove waste and therefore cost by removing time.

Since then I've applied this process in businesses as diverse as call centers and metals processing plants, and so far again in my experience, it has always achieved significant gains."

"Any thoughts?" I ask.

"We like it," the team echos back.

"I can't say it's the most often used tool in my toolbox," I say, "but it most certainly has its moments and one of them seems to be when we are on a path of getting more sales through our existing facilities and processes. I say sales because more unsold products would actually just cost us money as locked up inventory, so the trick will be to reengineer the processes when we create gaps of time in them. It will then be up to cross-functional teams from operations, sales, and finance to offer flexible pricing to new customers and to customers with high volume business with us when they take on additional volume."

"I'm glad I came today," says Linda.

"I'm glad you did too," I respond.

"What's next, Rory?" the team asks.

"I will go over the process with you one more time, developing diagrams that we can turn into worksheets, and then we go and apply it."

Date:_____   Process:_____

No.	WHAT	WHO							TIME	COMMENTS

Synchronous worksheet.

Worksite: Customer Support Services-CAC

Date: 8/10/94

Page: 2

Team:

What?	Who? Advisor	Customer	Service Manager	TAC	DSM	Supervisor	Dist.	Time	Comments
11 Advisor reviews case with DSM								1440 min (W) 3.1 min (Talk)	N.V.A.
12 Does the Advisor come to consensus with the DSM regarding the handling of the customer's concern									
13 Advisor reviews decision with Supervisor.								30 min (W) 30 min (Talk)	N.V.A.
14 Does Supervisor agree with decision/handling of case?									
15 Advisor contacts Service Manager and DSM and discusses case further advising all parties of CAC position.								18.5 min	N.V.A.
16 Advisor contacts customer to relay results of review.								8.67 min	V.A.

Example of synchronous in action.

Total Time: 2.115.24 min
Value-Added Time: 8.67 min
N.V.A Time: 2.106.57 min

33

Preliminary Meetings with the Owners and Presidents... The Faces behind the Deals

I have a heavy schedule over the next two weeks, the usual stuff at the office and the additional opportunity of having lunch with each of our high-profile targets for mergers and acquisitions. I have eight lunches booked, four in week one.

I arrive at a nice little steak house for my first meeting; it's in Cleveland! Quite a distance from our office in New York City. I guess I forgot to mention that these lunches take up pretty much one full day each! This is a meeting with the owners of the call center operation in South Africa, or should I say the empty call center. I've looked at the photographs and like them just fine, it's situated in a suburb forty-five miles outside Cape Town with good transportation to and from the business, which is a must when you will have up to one thousand employees to consider. The building itself is located on two floors above a shopping mall with an option on a third floor. It is kitted out for five hundred workstations, the telephony and the rest of the technology is pretty much state of the art, albeit a little over five years old. The work stations are a little small, but a long way from cramped.

The owners are a major player in the outsourced call center business and so a sometime competitor of ours. I know their president and our relationship has always been cordial, although I am on time he is already seated at the table when I arrive. He rises to greet me and reaches out with his hand.

"Hi, James, how are you?"

"I'm good, Steven, how are you?" I ask as we shake hands firmly.

"So you're interested in the call center in South Africa?"

"Yes, we don't have any offshore capability in our BPO division as yet and this could be a decent way of getting it. Why is it empty, Steven?"

"I thought you knew, James; we closed it down a month ago after parting company with a major client the business depended on. I hated like hell doing it, we had a great staff that performed well. Sometimes these things happen I suppose. You know South Africa I'm told; you used to have a company there a few years ago as part of one of your divisions, right?"

"Completely right, Steven; we hated closing that one too. It hangs over me still, call it a social conscience I suppose."

"The building is leased, right, Steven?" I ask.

"Yes and the equipment is owned and fully depreciated, so it won't be that hard to let go."

"What did you have in mind for value, Steven?" I ask.

"How does $10 million sound, James?"

"I understand why you might ask that amount, Steven; it seems like a nice site. Can you tell me how long the lease has still to run and whether or not there is a break fee to end it earlier?"

Steven smiles and shifts in his chair "I might be able to do it for a little less, the lease has five years to run and the break fee is $2 million decreasing with time."

"My guess, Steven, is that the fair market value of the work stations is quite low, they look locally made, and the handsets, computers, and telephony and supporting technology are at least five years old; it would be hard to sell. It would be great if you could sharpen your pencil regarding your ballpark price that is unless you have a client ready to move in who would come over to us with the transaction. If it fits all of our requirements after a due diligence we were thinking we would take over the lease and buy the assets."

Steven nods, "At this time we have no client ready to move in, but we are of course working on it. If you were buying the assets and taking over the lease when would it happen?"

"We don't have a client lined up either right now, Steven, so my guess is six months or more."

"If you could commit to six months we could do an asset sale and lease transfer for $5 million," Steven responds.

"Let me talk it over with the folks back at the ranch and I'll get back to you within the month. I can't make any commitments until after the due diligence, but that shouldn't take long if we go that far. I'll just fly a couple of our guys out to look at the assets and determine what the labor force situation is, that kind of thing. Our CFO would also need to talk to your CFO and then if everything pans out we will prepare a draft contract."

We shake hands and I head for the airport to catch a plane to Detroit.

I arrive early for my next luncheon appointment and admire the atmosphere in the cozy little Italian restaurant. There is a very convincing mural on the wall of Santorini surrounded by the blue of the Adriatic; I relax and can almost feel the sun on my face. "James?" a voice asks. I start and snap to attention. "Damn the Adriatic; it always does that to me," I mutter standing up.

My luncheon appointment laughs as he shakes my hand. "Heavy travel schedule?" he asks.

"I can't complain about it; I make my own schedule! Buddy Schwartz, I presume?"

"The very same," says Buddy still laughing. "Thanks for coming down to see me."

"It's my pleasure, Buddy." We sit down as the waiter walks over, "What's good here, Buddy?"

"Everything...but I like the spaghetti Bolognese."

"Good enough," I say, and we order two with some sparkling Pellegrino to drink.

"So, you are interested in buying our marketing business?" asks Buddy.

"Yes," I respond. "Like your business, ours is a conglomerate and this opportunity fits in with our automotive BPO business; it looks like it could be a good match. Can you tell me a little about it, Buddy?"

"Well as you know it supplies marketing services to most of the big automotive companies, quite a nice mix with the biggest share of any one client being 45%."

"So why does your company want to sell, Buddy?"

"Simple, really, James; it doesn't fit the core business. A few years back the then CEO bought a bunch of satellite companies to diversify us; some of them made sense and some didn't. Most of the divisions that didn't fit are now gone, this one is just about the last of any size."

"Can you tell me a little about the financials? Just high-level stuff really," I ask.

"I can, James, but I have to ask you to sign this confidentiality agreement."

I take it, read it, sign, and hand it back.

"The business operates from three locations, two of them here in Michigan and a third in California; our sales are approximately

$150 million per year, and we do not report each divisions profit within the conglomerate separately."

"Can you give me a ballpark as to how it does for profit, Buddy?"

After a short pause, Buddy responds, "It's losing about 7% per year."

I nod, "As a one-shot problem or as a general run rate?"

"It never quite met its potential inside our conglomerate, so you could consider this our normal run rate."

"And what about a selling price?" I ask, "Have you thought about it?"

"We have, James," says Buddy. "How do you feel about one times sales?"

I remain unruffled, "That strikes me as a high ask given the business is losing around $10 million a year, Buddy." And I wait for a response.

Buddy shrugs, "It seems fair to us, James; it has a good client list and lots of potential."

"Well, Buddy…I'll take it back to the folks at the ranch for consideration, but I have to say I don't think it will fly. We would be taking on a high degree of risk at this price. Before we could turn a profit we would have to turn it around to the extent of $10 million on the bottom line very quickly. Even if we did this in the first year of ownership it would still only be a break even business."

Buddy remains quiet.

"I'd like to do something with you on this one Buddy, at least move on to the due diligence stage to determine the practicability of going ahead… But before wasting either of our time and energy I think we need to know if you are flexible on the price."

"There could be some flexibility, James."

"Ok then, Buddy," we stand and shake hands. "We'll get back in touch with you real soon," and I leave for the airport.

My last two meetings this week are back on my home turf, so I'm heading back to New York State. My first lunch date is in Rochester and I'm meeting Charles Morales, the owner operator of Morales Transportation. We meet in an upper-end roadhouse, great ambiance and great burgers; I love that. Charles is already at a table when I arrive and he stands to shake my hand.

"I'm pleased to meet you, James," he says.

"I'm pleased to meet you too, Charles," I smile.

"Please call me Charlie; everyone does," and he smiles back while giving me an almost bone crushing handshake.

The food is great, the conversation is amiable, and we take our time getting down to business.

"Are you doing a lot of these this week, James?"

"I am," I respond and I find myself giving Charlie a more in-depth view of our company's plans than I thought I would. He is listening intently.

"Tell me about your company, Charlie."

"Well, my father started the business fifty years ago and nurtured it as his child until his retirement. Let me hasten to add he also nurtured me," Charlie's easy smile is ever present.

"I worked in the business from my late teens forward, as a driver, foreman, and then manager. My dad retired twenty years ago and I've ran the business ever since. We've had more good years than bad, but things have slowed down of late and our capacity is underutilized; we both know what that means."

"I understand, Charlie; business certainly takes its twists and turns." I can't help but sympathize.

"Tell me a bit more about the actual company, if you will, Charlie."

"We own our fleet, all sizes and types of vehicles, a good mix for our current very diverse business; we transport everything from steel to paper, to food stuffs. Some of the fleet is getting quite old but everything is well maintained; we have our own garage and service department. All of our buildings are leased and we operate over a large part of the country, not so much out west though."

"What do your financials look like?" I ask.

"Not great, James. At 100% utilization we make good money, but we are operating at 70% and that doesn't cut it."

"Is your name still good?" I ask.

"It is. Most of our customers are long term and have stayed with us, and it seems they are just shipping less by road. Also one or two have gone under."

"What are your current sales, Charlie?"

"Around $90 million."

"If you sell the business, how much would you hope to get and how would you like to be paid?"

"I love the business, James, and of course I'd like a fair price, but there is more to consider than money. We are a family business and I want to do right by our people and customers."

"Would it be your intent to stay on with the company?" I ask.

"I'd like that," Charlie smiles, with a hint of emotion in his eyes, "but it's a little more than I hoped for. I know there's a view out there that those who break it will not likely be the ones who fix it."

"There's truth to that line of thought, Charlie, but it's not always true or for that matter not always fair. Sometimes things actually do happen that are out of our control. If together we see a strong future for your company we can set up part of the payment over time based on results, this should give you good options I think. Can I get my folks in to start the due diligence?"

"You can, James, and thank you." We shake hands and part as friends.

I actually slept in my own bed last night; it's always nice to get home. My final meeting for this week is in the office, the founder and operator of Wonderful Chocolates has come all the way from San Francisco to meet with me, I'm honored. After a brief walk around the office and an introduction to the team we head out to the restaurant for lunch.

"Welcome to New York, William."

"Call me Willy, it kind of works out with the business name really, don't you think?"

"Willy's Wonderful Chocolates! I laugh out loud; it reminds me of a movie."

"It reminds everyone of a movie, James; I'm about as subtle as a sledge-hammer! But tell me, why on earth would you be interested in a business as small as mine, you are a huge conglomerate?"

"Small can be beautiful Willy, and in this day and age quite frankly we are not that huge...Tell me why you want to sell?"

"The business is my life's work, James, it's grown quite a bit since I started it half a lifetime ago. I'm a chocolatier, it's my chosen profession. However, I am no longer a young chocolatier and it's time to unlock some of the value I've built in over time; it's really that simple."

I smile, "things are seldom that simple; tell me more about your business if you will, Willy."

"We are headquartered in San Francisco and have ten shops across the West; all of them are successful, each grossing sales of approximately $500,000 per year; we make the best chocolate in the world; everyone loves us, even the Belgians and they are hard to please when it comes to chocolate. Each of the shops also responds to web sales, the numbers are built into the total, so we are in essence, if you will excuse the almost pun, a sweet $5.0 million business."

"How about profit levels, Willy?"

"Cost of goods run about 40%; we use only the best. The rest of our costs are wages and leases, again we have top quality locations so the lease cost is a little high. All of our assets and equipment are already fully depreciated."

"And what about profit my friend?" I ask again.

"There's the rub," Willy responds, "there isn't any! By the time all is said and done each year there might be around $700,000 left after all costs except my wages; I pay myself that." It may seem an excessive amount but it seems to be what my lifestyle has grown to, mine and the four kids, wife and ex-wife that is…."

We look at each other smiling a rueful smile, not so much a joyous one.

"How much do you hope to get for the business, Willy?"

"Maybe $4 million, James?" Willy asks hopefully.

"I'm going to send a couple of guys to see you and to spend a little bit of time in your shops; they will be invisible to your customers. As you know, we must do our due diligence. Regarding price, I can't say anything until after the due diligence has been completed. Would you be interested in staying on?"

"Absolutely," says Willy.

"Our current thoughts would be to wrap your Wonderful Chocolates in with our food and beverage division, but you would lead your business and be the best chocolatier in the world still. If we achieve agreed upon sales targets, we will do everything in our power to ensure all of your personal goals are achieved."

"Thanks, James," says Willy smiling, "I believe you are an honorable man."

"As I believe you to be also, Willy."

We part company both satisfied with the visit and my first series of luncheon meetings are complete. A good week!

34

And More Preliminary Meetings

I have four more preliminary meetings this week, quite an easy week really! First I'm off to Colorado to meet with a senior executive from a major packaging company to talk about buying a can plant, then I'm heading to Toronto, Canada, for a meeting with a pharmaceutical company, and back to New York for two video-conference meetings with the presidents of an automotive parts company in China and another in Mexico; what could be easier?

I arrive in Colorado and of course our meeting is in a grand steak house, apparently the special is something else: if you eat the whole thing you get it for free and if you can't finish it the staff all get together and ridicule you.

"I'll have the special please," I ask.

My lunch companion doesn't quite know how to react to that...

"Do you have any idea how big that steak is, James?"

"I have to think it's probably just a little thing," I respond.

"It hangs over the side of the plate all the way round and it's got to be an inch thick, what are you thinking?" asks my lunch partner.

"I'm thinking lunch, could I have it medium well please?" and off goes the waiter.

My lunch appointment laughs, and orders a salad. His name is Tim and he's a mountain of a man, the COO of a global packaging firm.

"So you want to buy one of our can plants, James?"

"I do Tim, I understand that you are consolidating your global manufacturing and are considering idling one of your older plants in New Jersey."

"That would be correct, James; it's always a difficult decision to idle a location."

"I agree Tim, lots of jobs at stake; maybe we can help there."

"Do you know the high-speed packaging industry at all, James? One line can turn out more than 1.5 million cans a day and they tend to run 52 weeks a year; what in the name of god would you do with all of those cans?"

"We have two opportunities, Tim: convert one of your two lines to a 12-ounce food line and pack our own products for our food divisions; the second line can stay on beer and beverage and we can co-pack our own product lines for those also."

"You do know a little about the can industry then," says Tim, "but that still won't use the full potential of both lines."

"Yes I know a little; as far back as 1986, I was a plant manager in a can plant for one of your competitors. My understanding is that your plant is kitted out with Standun B3 body makers, minster cuppers, Rutherford decorators, all good equipment to which you have applied high-speed packages and retrofits over the years. I know it's an old plant and likely long since fully depreciated; I also know the equipment is likely still sound."

The food arrived some time ago and I've already eaten half my steak as we talk; Tim stares at his salad and at the diminishing wonder on my plate.

"You are a very interesting man, James. How can we make this work?"

"I understand you are currently down to running one shift per day, if we both take half the production we can save the plant from being idled and help out a lot of families in New Jersey. This should save you quite a bit in redundancy payments; I guess you have had a lot of the folks in the plant for as much as twenty-five years. It's also a very good thing to show your other employees, it speaks volumes for a company that obviously cares."

Tim nods his agreement; I have all of his attention…half on my proposition and half on the steak that is now three quarters gone.

"What about the business side, the financials and management?" Tim asks.

"We will buy 50% of the plants assets at fair market value and pay 50% of all other costs, labor, lease, etc., all contingent on a successful due diligence of course. We intend to continue to grow our food and beverage business aggressively, and as we are able to take more and more of the plant's production volume, we will pay for more of the assets and other costs in proportion. Eventually, you can phase out your clients and consolidate them into your other plants for a complete exit."

"I'm impressed with your solution, James. Also, where the hell are you putting that steak?"

I continue to eat.

"Can I send our COO in to look at the can plant? He also used to run one, and can I have our CFO set up a time to talk with your CFO, Tim? I think this should be an easy due diligence for both of us."

"I'll talk with our CEO, James, and get back to you, but I agree with you this should be quite easy."

I eat my last forkful of steak.

"How the hell did you do that?" Tim asks.

"Easy Tim, I was hungry."

My flight lands at Pearson International in Toronto; I've spent a lot of time in this city over the years and made a lot of good friends, one of them is here to meet me at the airport today...my old buddy Peter.

"Hi, James, it seems like a long time," says Peter giving me a manly hug.

"Good to see you, Peter, what have you been up to?"

"Oh not much, a quiet life really, I just turned sixty. Where would you like to go for lunch?"

"Is the Armadillo still open?"

Peter laughs, "Oh god the times we spent there; what did we call the place back in the day...? The Armageddon!"

We take a cab into the city and laugh about old times in Toronto talking all the way about good times and bad. Twenty five years ago, we just had to go out on the town drinking together every Friday night that we could.

"So tell me about your life today, buddy." I say.

"I'm still happily married and I'm still excited about the world, still running, diving, and traveling off the beaten path."

We settle into the Armadillo and order Guinness and steak and kidney pie. "Do you want to sell your business, Peter?"

"Yes, I think so...time passes fast and nobody lives forever."

I nod, "It takes a long time to come to that conclusion, old buddy old pal," I say pensively.

"Tell me what's going on with the company now."

"Well, you know that I went out on my own after lots of years working for the big pharmaceuticals and built up a nice little generic pharmaceutical business; all the stuff you buy over the counter and some expired patented stuff to stop aches and pains, from pills to powders to liquids and we've done pretty well."

Peter is understating things; it's his way. In truth he is a genius with degrees in chemistry and science and a PhD; he even found the time to get his MBA.

"How is the business performing now, Peter; how much do you want for it?"

"The generic side is performing quite well, we could get a little more throughput I think, and I certainly believe we could sell the additional product we could produce when we do. You know of course we bought a company that produces vitamins, omega fatty acids and all that stuff? Well...we have never fully integrated it into the core business since we moved it into our facility. The truth is I don't want to work sixty-plus hours a week anymore."

"What are the annual sales mate?" I ask.

"The whole business is now at $200 million running at a blended 12% EBIT; the vitamin side is pulling the total EBIT down a little."

"What's the bank debt, buddy?" I ask.

"We have a long-term debt of $20 million."

"What do you think the business is worth today, Peter?" I ask.

"About $200 million minus the debt," Peter responds. "You and I can get a lot more out of it if I stay on!"

"Will you stay on?"

"As a consultant I will."

"Will you take some of the final price we agree as an earn-out over five years? If we go ahead that is."

"You'll pay me a consulting fee as well I hope?" laughs Peter.

"Of course," I reply.

"Then an earn-out is good; it will help even out the tax burden."

"I'll organize some of our guys to come and work with your guys on the due diligence then."

Peter drives me back to the airport. "This should be our opportunity to have a few beers together from time to time going into the future," he says.

"It better be" I laugh "It's been great, Peter."

Next day back at the office I finish my second week of meet and greet with the presidents of two automotive parts manufacturers: one in Mexico and one in China; thankfully we can do this on back-to-back video conference. They both go well as we all have the same agenda. To leverage off each other's automotive businesses, clients, and geographies, we discuss terms at a high level as being proportionate to what we, each of us, put in and deliver and agree to go ahead with a due diligence before we go any further.

I have to say when all of this is over that I am a combination of exhausted and exhilarated. I stroll along and drag John and Billy out of their offices and head downstairs for a coffee.

"How did it go?" asks John.

"Good I think," I reply.

"What's it going to cost?" Billy asks.

"Not too much," I respond. "How about we get together tomorrow?"

35

Go/No Go...Do These Ones Fit

We have everyone here in the board room; it's time to talk turkey. We have Smithy from projects, John representing ops, and Billy for finance. We also have sales, HR, communications, and IT. Rory is here and he has brought along his four analysis and continuous improvement team leaders. Oh...and legal, we can't forget legal. I go over the results of my meetings from the last two weeks with the team. Also in the room with us is Jane Austin, our M&A intermediary.

"So what do you think?" I ask the room.

"It all sounds very productive," says John, "doesn't sound like you broke a single thing."

Billy speaks up, "I'm trying to do the math in my head as you speak and it doesn't seem to come close to $1 billion."

"No...its way short," I agree. "Let's see what we think it looks like," and Rory picks up the pen.

	Projected Revenue	Projected Cost
The automotive marketing company	$150 million	$70 million
The pharmaceuticals and vitamins	$200 million	$180 million
The can plant	$50 million	$25 million
The transportation company	$90 million	$40 million
The call center in South Africa	$30 million	$4 million
The chocolate company	$10 million	$3 million
The two automotive partnerships	$20 million	$10 million
Totals	$550 million	$332 million

We all stop to look at the board. "Where are you getting some of these assumptions, James," asks Bill.

"Well as far as the projected cost side goes, the can plant, transportation company, and call center are asset buys, the automotive partnership is a guess, the marketing company is a turnaround, as to some degree is the pharmaceuticals, and the chocolate company is current fair market value.

The revenue side is pretty much what they told me, the big assumptions being the call center and the can plant because we supply our own business and clients for them. The chocolate company is what we should be able to build it to in year one and the automotive partnerships is a reasonable minimum expectation against the cost. We should fully expect to get more synergies though as we blend everything with our existing divisions."

Bill smiles, "OK."

"What do you think the sequence should be?" asks Smithy.

"I think (1) automotive marketing, (2) pharmaceuticals, (3) call center, (4) transportation company, (5) automotive partnerships, (6) chocolate company. However circumstances might well change the sequence and that's ok."

"Who should look at what," asks Rory.

I'm thinking out loud, "Legal, HR, IT, and finance should look at everything except the call center and the chocolate company, although come to think of it, finance and legal must look at absolutely everything as should HR. John, you and Rory should have someone on everything with both of you signing off on the findings."

"What are the next steps?" asks legal.

"Each function should draw up its specific due diligence checklist and be prepared to share it with the entire team. Then Smithy will work with each of you to determine the schedule. I hope to complete each on-site due diligence within two weeks of starting. Helen, could you prepare a communication for the board of directors? And Jane should continue the search for our second wave of acquisitions."

"Please remember everyone, one hidden or even obvious defect that we do not bring into the light for further consideration could kill us. The two biggest potentials for failure during the acquisition process are due diligence and integration."

36

Planning for the Coming Due Diligence

The team has arrived in the boardroom to go over the planning for the due diligence. I begin.

"It's generally thought that the two most important aspects of acquisitions are the due diligence and the integration. I certainly agree with that. If it's true that 95% of all acquisitions never realize all the synergies that were targeted, it simply underscores the need for caution and diligence at this stage of the process. So…the way I would like us to do this is to ensure that both the due diligence and the integration are seen as one item.

The way I propose we go about it is to take a leaf out of Rory's book and the information and experience he gained in the recent due diligence he conducted for us in Europe. Unfortunately, it did not lead to a deal but it did emphasize the point of not falling in love with an acquisition too quickly.

Rory, would you mind going over the lessons learned from Europe?"

"I'll be pleased to, James," says Rory, moving to the flip charts, and he creates a diagram as he goes along.

"We are going to analyze eight businesses over the next six weeks and this will entail a lot of work for all of us. It might well be tempting to ask for the information we require and go over it back at our office. I strongly recommend against it. We should have a presence on the potentials site for approximately two weeks during the due diligence phase, if possible let's make it no more than that. One week might do in the case of the chocolate company. Its small and likely very straightforward; this is also likely true for the call center as it's empty and we are looking at assets. However, all of the others deserve the time it will take us to grind things out. It's a good idea not to be alone on the prospects site if possible. It can be quite surprising what any one of us can pick up that another may miss; we should take advantage of that fact."

"But what if only one of us is needed for the task, Rory?" asks HR.

"Try to pair yourself up from a timing perspective with operations or sales or IT; otherwise we will lose the opportunity to leverage off each other. The primary reason for actually being there is that you never know where a great piece of information or for that matter a deal breaker will pop up. In my own experience I've often found the most important information shows itself that way.

We will be asking lots of questions and observing people as they go about their work. We have sixteen folks who have become quite expert at that during the last few months and they are available to work with you across all of the functions. Their skills are process related as well as content related and so they are flexible and transferable to the due diligence, and these good folks want to help and learn from you too.

You can see I'm drawing a masterpiece on this flip chart as we talk, I'm trying to take the words that are flying through the air and capture them in a plan, a plan where all the elements interrelate with each other. I am drawing it in four quadrants, but you can see I'm leaving enough room at the bottom of the chart to create a fifth, sixth, seventh, or even eighth category. I guess I'm a fly-by-the-seat-of-my-pants kind of guy! Please help me with it, if we get it right it should represent what we want from an acquisition and set us on the road to getting it."

Now the body language is poised in the forward position.

The analysis quadrants/categories	
Finance	Customers
Operations	HR
Management	IT
Strategy	Legal

"The first quadrant is financial, what is the business worth?"

- What are the total sales dollars?
- What is the operating margin?
- What is the EBIT?
- What is the monthly/annual performance as compared to budget?
- What is the debt to equity ratio?
- What are the support costs, sales, general, and administration?
- Show all of this in graph form for the last five years.

- Are there onetime costs or sales, where are they?
- Is the business seasonal?
- What are the inventory turns?
- What is the total value of the inventory?
- Is there inventory that is slow moving or out of date?
- What is the free cash flow?
- What are the days due on payables?

I've already abandoned the one flip chart deal and am posting a complete sheet to support each quadrant on the wall.
The next quadrant is customers.

- What percentage of sales does each customer represent?
- What are each major customers buying patterns?
- Who are our key relationships and supporters in each client company?
- What does each say about us as a company face to face?
- How is our largest customers sales performing (growing, stable, declining)?
- Show the key customer information on graphs over the last five years.

The next is operations.

- Do operations have production/performance targets for each day?
- How do they measure productivity?
- How do they measure throughput?
- How do they address downtime?
- How do they solve problems?
- What is their on-time and complete delivery performance?
- What is their waste/scrap/rework percentage and cost?
- What is the total cost of the work in process (WIP)?
- Is there reliance on overtime?

The next is HR.

- Are any of the employees represented by a union?
- Has there been any industrial action over the last five years?
- What is the management performance system?
- How is the culture described by the executive? Management? Employees?

- How does the culture look to you?
- What is the grievance record, are there any grievances outstanding?
- Are all pensions funded/accrued for?
- What is the vacation and time off policy?
- Are there regulations affecting overtime?
- Are there any pay for performance programs in place?
- What is the lateness, absenteeism, and attrition performance?
- Graph the key indicators over the last five years.

The next is management.

- Is management passive or active?
- Do you see management on the floor actively solving problems?
- How effective is the chain of command?
- Is there demonstrated responsibility and accountability for performance?
- How do the management meetings work?
- How are the managers incented?
- Do any particular managers stand out for good or bad?
- What is the extent of management turn over?

Next is IT.

- Are their systems compatible with ours; does it matter?
- Is the technology stable and effective as a standalone?
- Is any of the technology out of date/redundant?
- To what extent will we have to upgrade the technology?
- Should we partially or completely integrate the technology?

Next is strategy.

- Is there a current strategic document?
- What does the strategy tell us regarding direction over the coming three to five years?
- Does the annual budget reflect the strategy?
- Is the strategy reviewed and progressed/actioned at regular intervals?
- Is the strategy understood throughout the organization, to what levels?

James steps up, "This list is generated by a generalist, not someone who is a specialist in each function, and so we know it is incomplete. I ask you to complete the high-level list for your function to fill in the blanks you see here and let us see it. Please remember that our objective here is to grow our business by acquisition and so we want the businesses we are looking at to work out, but don't fall in love with them! If there are aspects of them that are broken please consider how to fix them, but any fixes we have to make should be considered in the price we finally pay for the business.

During the due diligence and the subsequent integration, Rory will be in charge so please keep him up to date daily on any key issues you see. Always look for the deal breaker; better to find it now rather than later, even if it disappoints us. We should all meet here for a debrief on the entire due diligence at the close of the second week, please allow two hours for this meeting."

37

Details for the Due Diligence...
Questions...Questions...Questions

The teams are back in the room and they have a spokesperson; it's Linda from HR.

"Well, James, we were listening to you and we thought it was a good idea to get into team mode on this straight away. Rory was onboard with the idea and so we met as a team, reviewed all of the inputs from the previous meeting, and simply brainstormed all additional items together, regardless of which functional group any item belonged to. And so here's the list...this is strictly an eyes open endeavor and so if we've missed anything it will be sought out as we go."

- Org charts for the entire business down to team and operator level. We will be looking for opportunities in span of control.
- Analyze customer base for negative buying patterns and sentiment.
- Age and condition of facilities and equipment.
- Contract analysis regarding employees, customers, and vendors.
- Purchasing procedures.
- Examine past and projected CAPEX spending.
- Graph all major quantifiable elements in each function over the past five years.
- Examine the functionality of all hardware and software.
- Examine the companies tax situation and filings for the past five years.
- Perform physical inventory count and ensure it is properly valued.
- Graph and analyze all major financial ratios for the past five years.
- Review curriculum vitaes of all senior management.
- Perform a competitor analysis.

- Perform a SWOT analysis of all functions—Strengths, Weaknesses, Opportunities, Threats.
- Analyze breakdown, changeover, repairs, and maintenance logs.
- Graph and analyze each department's expenditures for the past five years.
- Identify and examine all past and outstanding litigation.
- Review any available audits for the past five years.
- Analyze the company's sales and marketing strategy for the coming five years.
- Analyze the respective profit levels for each category of business and each major client.
- Analyze all employee incentive plans.
- Read the board minutes for the past five years.
- Examine the accounting policies.
- Examine accounts payable and associated accruals.
- Analyze forward projected gross profit by major category and client.
- Status of any patents.
- Analyze employee relations for the past five years.
- Analyze balance sheets for the past five years.
- Examine for any outstanding environmental issues.
- Graph and examine cash flow for the past five years.

Rory stands up and addresses me and the room, "We know this list is a bit thin, barely thirty items and a bit jumbled up to the casual eye. We also understand that there are items here that have to be broken down into their component parts; Smithy is going to help us with that. There will be a complete project plan tailored to each of the eight due diligences we intend to conduct. There will be elements of work, precedence relationships, timelines, and accountabilities, and there will be a performance review at the close of day every day to ensure we are all on the same page."

"All sixteen members of our internal analysis team will be seconded to these due diligence practices until their completion; they are now trained and experienced analysts and will apply all the skills and know-how they have gathered through helping us optimize our existing business. We are one team and although for many of us this will be our first due diligence all of us are experts in our existing functions. We know what we will be looking for and our goals and project plans will simply be tools that keep us on focus. We know that as a company we would dearly like each of these targeted opportunities to be a part of our company, but we are not married to any of them; heck we haven't even fallen in love with any of them yet. We understand that just like there is always a nut to be cracked to open up opportunities in any business there is also a potential hidden elephant trap that we could fall into and be swallowed up by in any business we intend to acquire. We all love our company; we have worked hard to optimize it so that we could confidently go down this path of mergers and acquisitions. We will not squander our gains on any lukewarm opportunity, we will be ever vigilant in our search for the elephant trap and if we see any we will either circumvent it through our combined genius or we'll walk away! We're good James."

James thanks us and expresses his confidence. John says, "Ha...who accused any of you of being a genius?" then he stands up and addresses James.

"We get the key tenets, James: no acquisitions that don't complement our existing business, everything to be accretive within the first financial year of ownership, ensure we always get the best legal and accounting advice, and find the killer elephant traps in advance."

"He speaks," says Rory.

38

The Due Diligence Is Launched

We are having a pre-meeting with the entire analysis team, all of the senior department heads are present plus the teams they intend to deploy during the analysis. Also present are the sixteen trained analysts and continuous improvement experts from our in-house team. The objective of this meeting is to get an agreement of what we will be looking for during the due diligence process. John and James are also present but the outcome and the subsequent outputs of this meeting are clearly my responsibility.

James opens the meeting, "Hello, everyone, you are about to embark on one of the most important elements of the M&A process; you have done your prep work and you are ready. Now Rory will lead you through the final details, as you know he has accepted responsibility for the overall output not only of the due diligence but of the integration and the achievement of the synergies. I need you all to respect each other and the leadership that Rory will provide in this endeavor; please go ahead, Rory."

"Hi, everyone...We really appreciate you being here today and the commitments that you have already made to this process. It seems odd to talk about what you are doing here as a process and yet it most certainly is, the fact that it is a process doesn't make it a wooden venture, it's the opposite of that. It is a dynamic series of steps that lead us to a worthy goal. The goal of the due diligence is to ensure the companies we examine together meet our requirements to grow and diversify our current business to ensure that we achieve our targeted top-line sales and EBIT targets with an acceptable level of risk.

We decided at the outset of this exercise that any businesses we targeted for possible acquisition would already be related to our core capabilities in some defined way, and so there are no unrelated businesses among the eight we will be examining. The pharmaceutical and chocolate companies will bring new product lines to our food and beverage business as well as increase our geographic reach in Canada; the automotive marketing business and call center in South Africa will expand the offerings from our BPO business and offer a lower cost-blended solution to our clients through expanded product and service offerings and the benefits of offshore labor arbitrage, not only in the automotive sector but in all our other related clients businesses, including Telco and Financial services. The partnerships in automotive manufacturing will give us reach into expanding markets in China and Mexico where we can benefit from expanding our offerings to include cost-effective subassemblies through offshore labor arbitrage. The partnership with the can company will allow us cost reductions in our expanding requirements for aluminum cans for our beverage business and steel cans for our food business and it is also a natural fit with our metal distribution and processing business. The transportation business will allow us to link all of our companies transportation needs together, from our suppliers to us and from us to our customers.

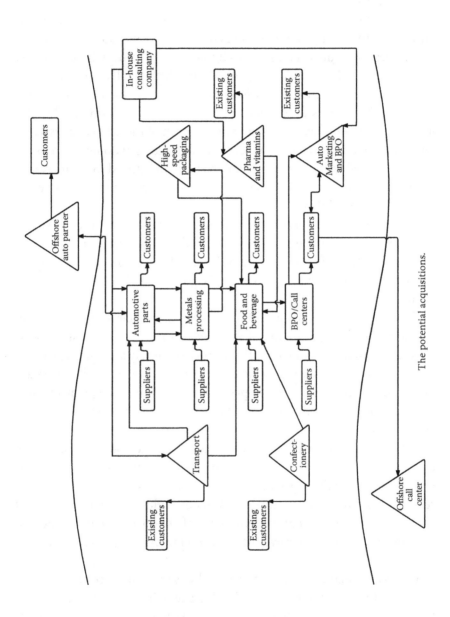

The potential acquisitions.

Most of our targeted businesses bring with them their own existing clients with some crossover to our existing client base. If we can keep and grow the existing clients each brings to us while having them also serve our existing clients we will achieve very real synergies. If any existing or new business within our group has an open market for its goods and services that values its products and services it must succeed through maximizing the application of its two flexible assets from which it will offer these goods and services. It has time and it has space...24 hours each day and seven days a week when its products can flow through its existing facilities to its customer base. If we can expand one or both of these flexible assets we take advantage of the fact that most of our fixed costs of doing business are already covered with only the variable costs being applied to the increased production volume we can achieve. This of course exponentially increases our overall profitability.

We set out on this venture to do exactly these things, to increase our overall business from $1.5 billion to $3.0 billion and our earnings before interest and taxes from 8% to 12%. If any of the businesses we will be analyzing fail to move us toward this goal then that business is not for us.

It's widely believed that most businesses that are acquired do not meet the targeted synergies; many of them in fact deplete the existing business as opposed to adding to it, this is most definitely a luxury we cannot afford. It's at this crossroad where due diligence leads to the purchase of a related business at a good price and then the subsequent integration of that business into the core business that we ensure the targeted synergies are achieved.

Not all synergies are financial in nature and yet at the end of the day they must meet the financial targets that have been set. And so when you are analyzing management, employees, operations, human resources, finance information technology, sales and marketing, and legal, you must see them as being part of the puzzle that will add to our ability to achieve our overall financial targets as opposed to detract from them.

A well-executed due diligence paves the way for a successful integration. What you find during the due diligence will not always be an exact fit to our requirements; when it is not, we have to visualize how our efforts can make it so. If this is not possible, we may have found the deal breaker, the elephant trap that if we inadvertently fall into could make us a statistic in the failed acquisition league. So here is the conundrum, do not fall in love with the business too soon and yet be wide open to changing your view if you see the potential.

So it's back to the process, we have clearly defined project plans for each business we will analyze; these will be our road map. As you focus on completing each step in the process keep your peripheral vision on everything else that is going on around you, the best information often pops up from a seemingly casual conversation or observation so be open to it. The output of the completion of each step should therefore be a go ahead, a deal breaker, or a provisional go ahead where we know what we have to do to by-pass any potential shortfall in performance.

I encourage everyone to consider the high level requirements of the project first, know whether or not each step you are looking at in each function can meet the minimum requirements of the project and if it does not, then bring it up immediately at the end-of-the-day team meeting. Don't get immersed in the detail until you know that the big picture works.

"When it comes to the amount of time each of us must spend on the due diligence, it should be as much as required, not as much as you think you can spare. If you can't finish it you shouldn't start it… As a rule of thumb functional leaders should be prepared to spend at least 50% of their time on the due diligence while maintaining their responsibility within the core business, this will tax you but it is only for a relatively short time, all eight of the due diligence's will be more or less running in parallel and so they should be completed within a month or so from start to finish. Each of us must select good, capable, and willing alternative substitute players for ourselves when we are absent. I can see each of you have largely already done that.

At the close of the due diligence, we will consolidate our findings off site; the on-site work should be kept to within two weeks. Once consolidated, we can request any information we may have missed, our findings will then be presented to James, John, and Bill, at this stage there should be no surprises as we will be reporting up to them at least weekly as we progress.

At the point of the final presentation, we should have firm recommendations in place that are backed up with hard facts. We should also be presenting a first blush integration plan at that time.

The integration plan should be supported by a project plan addressing each functional outcome against a predetermined timeline. Each of the due diligence teams will also have a degree of responsibility for the final integration of each business. Who better to guarantee the success of the mission than the people who analyzed and planned it; we must be prepared to hold each other accountable.

Finally, a successful integration does not necessarily mean that the acquired business takes on the same identity as the acquiring business. We should strive to take on the best of each other's culture and capabilities, not submerge them. It is not necessary to duplicate the chain of command, replace the IT platform, or implement new policies and procedures unless there is a real benefit in doing so. Some acquired businesses are best suited to stand alone or be partially integrated, depending on their nature.

Any questions?"

"When do we start?" I hear from sales.

"In one week," I say. "Be ready folks."

There is what appears to be a protracted silence; it's probably less than a minute though it seems like an hour, it's not uncomfortable, and in fact it's filled with energy.

"James, John, Billy, do you have any closing thoughts?"

John pipes up, "I'll work with you between the companies; I'm in it with you."

Bill says, "Same here, although it's important for John and I to keep a low profile as far as the clients and the current business ownership is concerned, we should be in reserve for escalations and potential deal breakers."

James is exhibiting the ultimate in calmness, "I have never been so confident in anyone or any endeavor in my life as I am with you and this one. Bon chance!"

39

In the Final Analysis

There are none of the big stars here anymore, James and John have exited themselves from this particular meeting; there is no chairman of the board, there is just me, Rory, the great and powerful Oz. Well not exactly, there is me and the thirty-six people who will have the keys of the kingdom in their hands, the due diligence team. There are so many of us we are sitting in rows just as if we are back in school.

I break the silence, "Anyone nervous?" I ask.

There's some laughter and a few strained comments, everyone is trying to keep it light and yet most of all there is silence.

"I'm nervous, Rory," says Linda, the VP of sales. "Is that a bad thing?"

"Nothing is good or bad other than our thinking makes it so, Linda," I respond.

"Oh god, he's philosophizing again," chirps out one of my team.

"Give the lad a chance!" says another, and they all laugh with a little more sincerity, but hardly with exuberance.

The thirty-six people in the room are made up of each of the corporate department heads each with at least one trusted assistant, I say assistant and yet these good folks are all senior, they are the best of the best in each functional group in our company. Twenty content experts assisted by sixteen of my team of trained and experienced analysts.

"The nervous thing…," I say, "Sir Laurence Olivier was asked if he still got nervous before going on stage. He responded that he got nervous every time, and when that nervousness went away he would know he was done! Embrace your nervousness; it's there for a reason."

"We've got to get out of this room and quickly," I state. "The longer we stay in the safety of corporate we are simply navel gazing, theorizing. It's hard for me to cut the cord and get into the field on this one there is so much at stake, but I have to, we have to. So this is a temporary goodbye, to a large extent I'm leaving each of you to it."

Complete silence.

"You know your teams and by and large you know each other, we will conduct eight formal due diligence processes and there will be approximately four core people in each team. Each will be almost simultaneous with approximately two weeks between the beginnings of the first to the end of the last; each will aim for a maximum of two full weeks on site with the prospective acquisition. Any time lag is designed to allow for travel over the somewhat wide geography we have to cover, each core groups team leader has a projected start time for your particular on-site work. Smithy has worked up the sequencing in a flow chart to ensure travel time and the needed expertise availability will all fit into our schedule. There will be jet lag involved for those who visit China, Europe, and South Africa; we have figured in as much recuperation time as possible to lessen the impact of this, but it's a reality in a global company."

I stop to draw breath and there are questions.

"Can we break company policy and go business class on these long hauls?"

"Yes to China and South Africa, no to Europe. We have to balance our comfort with the overall cost to the company and its effect on our annual budget expectations, everyone has a budget, and in fact there are budgets within budgets! For most of us, including me, we would travel to Europe in economy if we were on our own dime, it's a seven-hour flight, we have to treat the company as if it were our own and the budget as if it were our own money. We love you though and we need you strong, so Europe will be premium economy. I urge all of you to get as much rest during travel as you can, it will all be stressful enough."

"What about centering ourselves as a team prior to splitting up on site to conduct the actual analysis? And what about gathering our thoughts at the end of each analysis segment we conduct?"

"Where any of our divisions has a location close to the analysis site a conference room will be made available to you; if there isn't one then use one of your hotel rooms. You'll certainly need a day to gather as teams prior to setting foot on the prospects premises, the final-final so to speak. Each prospect will also be laying on an office for you to work in on site; that's where you should gather your thoughts between each phase of the operation and hold your end-of-day-findings meeting as a team. There will be times, however, that your judgment will tell you that certain meetings should be held off site; follow your intuition on that one."

"What if we find something we consider to be a deal breaker?"

"That's good and bad at the same time; I used to think that it was impossible for something to be both at the same time but I have learned that it certainly is not! It's good that you find that potential deal breaker early; we don't want to fall into the dreaded elephant pit after the deal is done and we are integrating the business and working to realize the financial targets and synergies.

It's bad because we want to do these acquisitions and we don't want to run away at the first whiff of smoke, so look at the problem objectively as a team and see if there is any way to turn it to our advantage. Consider if we could do something entirely or partially different than it is currently being done as a work-around. If not, then consider whether it might still be a good deal for us, but at a different price point than we first considered.

In all cases please get me into the loop as quickly as possible and we will decide whether we should get James, John, or Bill involved. We might abort the due diligence and get off site as quickly as possible or we might continue searching to determine whether there might be an offsetting advantage that we may have missed so far."

"Anything else?" I ask.

There's silence, it goes on for about a minute before I get the final question.

"What else is on your mind about this, Rory?"

"My head's buzzing just like yours is, so let me gather my thoughts with you on these flip charts; for some reason this always works for me, so in no particular order.

- Always use discretion; be careful how you talk with people and ensue you don't leave a bad impression or a false expectation.
- Don't leave your notes and papers lying around and make sure you clean off white boards and take down flip charts when you are not in the office.
- Be open to your gut feelings, your intuition. Look at the peripherals as to what's going on as well as the core things you are studying, whether as interviews, data analysis, or direct observations.
- Don't fall in love with the opportunity too quickly, always be on the lookout for that deal breaker.

- Begin with the end in mind; work out the equation as to how the sales and profit margin can meet our expectations. Examine to see what the extent of change will need to be to make this deal viable.
- Find and list the synergies that we wish to achieve to make the deal viable.
- Study all of the customer contracts; are we paid by the unit? Is it take or pay? What other methods are we paid by? Does this jive with the invoicing?
- Study all other contracts, including suppliers and employee, etc.
- Get out and talk to the customers; are they happy? Do they plan to stay with the company? How do they see their ongoing volumes of work from us?
- Talk to the suppliers and see if they expect any changes in pricing in delivery, etc.?
- Is there any litigation old or pending?
- Is there any risk from unionization?
- Look for what you are not being told.
- Have every core measure graphed over the previous five years and by month over the previous twelve months; look for trends and exceptional performance, good or bad.
- Study the strength of the management and senior leadership. Is the number two in each function capable of performing the work of the number one?
- Look at the utilization of the people who actually process the work toward completion. Can the work be reengineered? Can the cycle time be improved?
- Study the quality and downtime logs and compare it to what you see on the floor.
- Look at warehousing, components, and work in process; is any of it obsolete? Is it fat, sufficient, or insufficient to ensure smooth work flow and the meeting of customer shipments?
- Is there an expectation from the clients that they will receive price reductions each year?
- Are there special prices for volume in place?
- Are there health and safety risks, what is the attendance record and accident rate?
- Is there any expectation of increase in lease or other property costs?
- Are there necessary equipment upgrades and replacements?"

"What else?" Everyone is making notes as I am scribbling down the points. Silence!

"Meet with Smithy this week and ensure all of your project plans are in sync. Some of you plan to be involved in multiple due diligences. Make sure that's possible and that your functional deputies are capable of filling your spot when you are away from your core due diligence location. If not, plan to add additional resources now. Use the standard template we have developed to consolidate your findings for James, John, and Bill, show threats as well as opportunities and come to your conclusions.

I will visit every due diligence site with the exceptions of China and South Africa during the process. Smithy has my schedule for this as part of the overall project plan. Use me when I am there and call me if you need me when I am not. Any final questions?"

"No…I think we are good, Rory."

"OK…let's plan to be back in this room one month from now with our findings tabulated and we will review them together before presenting them to our company senior executive. The weekly due diligence updates as a full team will have to be by conference call; don't do these from the prospects site."

Cultural
Financial
Sales
Customers
Suppliers
Operations
Human Resources
IT
Legal
Facilities
Equipment
Strategy
Executives/Management
Five-Year Financial History/Trends
Five-Year Financial Projections
Other
Red Flags
Synergies/$ Value
Recommendations

Due diligence findings template.

40

The Numbers Are In

The team has completed their due diligence; they have thoroughly analyzed each company and have gone over them as a group with me and our four division presidents. I've asked James to join us for a formal debrief and he in turn has asked Alex to attend. So here we all are in the boardroom, thirty-six analysts representing all the functions in the business presenting to the company's senior executive and the chairman of the board. All of the due diligence team are a bit nervous, and so I begin.

"Thanks for being here everyone; it's our intention to use a standard format in presenting our findings on each business we reviewed. We will look at current and projected aspects of each element under review, which will include top-line and bottom-line performance, the major cost elements by category and our rationale around possible upsides and downsides to these numbers. We will highlight the major elements of synergy savings by business and their dollar amount, and finally we will look at threats and opportunities and our recommendations. With your blessing we will go over all eight business's one at a time in this manner, finally summarizing with all of them together. Lastly, we'll take questions and discuss next steps.

Is this agreeable to everyone?" It seems to be and so I hand things over to the first presenter. "Take it away please, Helen."

"Good morning everyone, although like most of us I've simply served with the other team members across many of the prospects we have decided, I'll present the findings on the automotive marketing company.

As you can see the current top line is $150 million and the profit line is (–$10 million) not acceptable to us as an acquisition as an ongoing business performance. However, if you look at the future state, the numbers change dramatically...they were achieved by beginning with the end in mind. We knew that to make this go forward we would need a bottom line improvement of 18% to get us to an EBIT line of 12%. So we re-jigged the numbers to reflect the art of the possible, and this you can see in the major cost and profit characteristics of the projected performance."

Everyone takes a little time to review the numbers; remarkably they all remain silent and allow Helen to continue.

We have identified an increase in the top line of 100% or $150 million; we expect this to be achieved from two sources; these being increases in volume to our existing clients of current services and the addition of our core customer and technical support competencies to these same existing clients.

We have also identified the likely transfer of the marketing and marketing analytic skills, which are a natural synergistic sell to our existing clients across our existing call center business. As you can see in the breakdown of these numbers, we expect to double the size of the business.

On the flip side to the happy numbers we have identified the need to reduce nondirect and support costs by 10% or $15 million; this is always difficult for everyone involved but we will do it carefully and fairly and as importantly; we will be seen to do it as such.

The analysis turned up no showstoppers although two clients make up 75% of the current business, the core automotive client and a major Telco. We met with senior executives across the entire client base and, in general, they are happy. The two red flags are likely requests for price reductions from the key automotive company and faster reconciliation of white mail issues from the major Telco client. If the requests are reasonable, we expect to be able to address them through process improvement.

The major synergies are as follows:

- Cross-pollination of the marketing skills to our existing clients.
- Cross-pollination of our customer care and technical assistance skills from our core business.
- Increased work from nonautomotive clients for our suites of product and services.
- Add new clients from both automotive and nonautomotive targets.
- Efficiency improvements across the business.
- Tiered pricing for new clients and price volume discounts.
- Nondirect and management cost reductions through layoff.

Our recommendation is that we go ahead with this acquisition.

There is a general nodding of heads from the audience and a warm thank-you for the work performed by the due diligence team. There is also a caution offered regarding the likelihood of a cost reduction request from our biggest automotive client.

"Next we would like to debrief the pharmaceutical opportunity and Lucy will present the findings. I hand it over to our strongest trained analyst; you wouldn't recognize her from the young woman who joined the analysis team from our food business twelve months ago. I have to admit I am proud of her and delighted to see how she carries her expanded skill set."

"Hello all, I'm Lucy Stevenson," she says smiling. "Prior to joining our in-house analysis team, I was a quality control manager with our food division, we believe this is a good acquisition and we should go ahead!"

Her face is beaming and she looks as though she is ready to sit down, obviously she thinks the one pager projected onto the screen tells the whole story! There's a moment of silence and then gentle laughter from many of the audience; it's all very catchy and soon the whole room is laughing out loud, so is Lucy; she remains completely unfazed.

I say with all the respect in the world, "Would you like to add anything else, Lucy?"

"Oh yes...yes...I'm happy to," she replies through her own laughter. "I worked on this due diligence with lots of other members of our team and with no small input from Rory. You see Peter the owner of the Pharmaceuticals is an old friend of Rory's and James's I believe, and he's a lovely man, he wants this to work as much as we do! There are no flaws in the business that would constitute a deal breaker, the only major danger we can see would be Peter moving on and setting up as a competitor, genius that he is, but he's staying! He just wants a little freedom to actually live his life and some money to do that with, so Rory, James, and Peter seem to have worked out exactly that.

Essentially Peter gets the money he wants with a large portion of it in the form of an earn-out. He continues to work for the company half time and ensures a comfortable transition over the next five years; everyone is happy with this deal, including the clients and customers.

We have the expertise to smooth out any production difficulties and any required tweaking to ensure a smooth integration of the new vitamins division. We also have the knowhow to improve overall marketing to grow our markets across Europe and the money to launch a brand named line of products in North America. We can integrate this business very nicely with our existing food and beverage business and sell from our chain of stores and those of others. It's a very sweet deal."

Lucy looks as though she is going to sit down again, but stops herself at the last minute as if she has just remembered something monumental. "Oh…you really have to meet Joan Wilson, the head of creative marketing at the automotive company we are just about to acquire!" There is more good humored laughter from the group, which elicits beaming smiles from Lucy. "She can help us with all of this, all one big plan phased over time. She's lovely…brilliant, in fact. This is a great business, we can easily triple it in size and meet and exceed all the profit targets!" With that, Lucy finally sits down, leaving the group to digest the information displayed on the screen.

Both James and Alex stand up and they are clapping; the whole room follows them, including the analysis team. James nods to Alex, who then speaks.

"I have to tell you I am highly impressed; good work everyone. This has the potential to be a jewel in the company's crown."

I thank the senior team on behalf of the due diligence team…and then I surprise one of them.

"John, would you mind doing the can plant?"

Our COO John walks out to the floor and gives me his usual wry grin, "You know fine well you could have done this one, or better still asked James to do it."

We both laugh, as does James, in way of explanation John addresses the room.

"Many moons ago we all worked together in the can making business, I was the big boss then…the plant manager. Unlike Rory's usual approach he is bending to convention and leaving it to the senior man to report out; James and I had the privilege of doing this particular due diligence with him. James conducted the preliminary meeting and then Rory and I went into the plant together and gave it the old eyeball. The boss would usually make this report, but back in the day James was the head of training and development and Rory was a shift manager, a couple of young whippersnappers really. As plant manager, I was the boss, so these two have cooked it up that I present today!"

"Well get at it then!" says James.

"One of the world's major can companies is consolidating, the International can company used to have locations serving pretty much the entire globe. Gradually, over the years, they morphed into the service sector, financial services, etc. During that time they sold off many of their international can-making divisions and pretty much consolidated what remained in North America. Although they are now happy with the percentage of their business that is still in manufacturing, the high-speed packaging industry has gotten even faster. It's more than impressive and in fact quite ingenious how can-making equipment that could print the cans at 1500 per minute twenty years ago can be retrofitted to get up to 2000 cans per minute. The cans coming off the decorator at this speed are just a blur to the casual eye, but the trained eye of the operator can focus on one can at a time and assess the quality of the print while it's on the run.

So whether it's brand new can-making equipment, from presses to wall ironers to decorators to inside spray machines, or for that matter the twenty-year-plus-old equipment that has been retrofit with high-speed packages, there is less and less of it required to fill the customer requirements. And so through our joint connections James, Rory, and I heard of the International Can Companies intention to mothball one of their older plants in New Jersey.

The can plant has two lines each capable of running at 1500 cans per minute, it is normal for these plants to run 24 hours a day 360 days a year, high-speed packaging just loves to run, it's when it's in stop–start mode that there's a problem.

We buy cans for our food and beverage business from one of their competitors right now and occasionally find ourselves facing price increases due to our being a relatively small client from their perspective, but we could consume half of the volume produced from both lines in this plant from one shift per day right now! As our intention is to grow our food and beverage business over the coming five years and beyond, we could gradually expand our can requirements to take on the entire shifts production, and later the production of the two additional shifts, which would normally run during the time the equipment is currently moth-balled."

Once again the room is silent, and then Alex speaks up, "I'm not a manufacturing guy and yet it seems to me that we will be carrying the costs of underutilized and idle equipment for some time, I don't understand how this could work to our advantage."

"You have James to thank for this one," says John. "He has proposed a very brilliant deal with International Can that will go ahead when blessed by our company's board of directors."

All eyes are on James, including those of Alex.

"I guess that's my cue," says James standing up and moving to the middle of the floor.

"First off, John and Rory guarantee that the equipment, although old, is in top-notch condition, and a plus side to twenty-year-old gear is that it is fully depreciated. The building is leased and the number of employees has been reduced by two-thirds over the years due to two of the three potential shifts being moth-balled.

International Can is concerned about their image in New Jersey, which is where the business began over one hundred years ago and so they would dearly love to leave this plant open, that's their motivation.

They are prepared to keep the plant running as it is now and absorb half of the production output we do not currently require and continue to meet the needs of some of their own customers from this location. They will make up the shortfall due to our taking a share of the output from their new locations, and as our capacity requirements increase they will gradually phase out their requirements from this location."

"Who takes on the responsibility for the employees?" asks Alex.

"We share it proportionately to our use of the plant's production levels. There are only twenty employees on the shift, but as we open up other shifts we can call back experienced can makers as well as train new ones."

"It sounds great," says Alex. "What does it mean to us financially?"

John picks up the conversation, "Right off the bat we will save 25% of our current cost of packaging for both food and beverage. One of the lines is tooled for 12-ounce aluminum beverage and beer cans and the other can be retooled as a steel food line for soup and vegetables.

The business starts out as a partnership with us carrying approximately 50% of the total costs of production, equipment, and facilities. Once our volume requirements match one shifts output we will complete the deal and take over the plant as an asset sale; due to the equipment's age it will be reasonably priced."

"What makes you believe you can double our current requirement for packaging? Doesn't that mean you intend to double the size of the food business?" asks Alex.

"That and more, Alex," says James. "We plan to go big box and international."

41

An Integrated Approach

Alex gives James a sideways glance; he's not sure if what he is feeling is admiration for James or wonder. Has he gone right over the edge? James nods to me and I get onto my feet again.

"It is probably obvious to everyone after seeing and hearing the first three presentations that we are following a mixed-bag approach to growing our business. All of it of course is contingent on getting our own house in order and this we continue to do showing what we believe to be remarkable results so far. We have also become very aware of the potentially high cost and possible risk of failure in growing through acquisition, and so caution has remained our watchword. So far we have shown you two acquisitions that are straightforward deals although the first requires a turnaround and the second is dependent on the ongoing involvement of the company's founder and an earn out as well as our expertise. The third we have shown you involves a partnership agreement and the future acquisition of assets. Each of these have many things in common, not least of all that they all fit into an overall plan of a new company that is tailor made to our existing business, also we've done them all on the cheap knowing that a company our size and composition couldn't easily afford the likely price of a 40% premium on a one times sales purchase of another existing publicly traded company.

What you are about to see is more of the same, caution in all things to produce a fully integrated business at a fair and reasonable price. Clive…could you present this one please?"

"Good morning, everyone. My name is Clive Oliver and it's my pleasure to stand here in front of you today. I have been part of the due diligence team and just like everyone else have spent some of my time on more than one of the targeted acquisitions, although the lions share has been on the one I'm about to present to you. My day job is as transportation manager for our metals distribution company, and oh yes...I've had the good fortune of working on Rory's analysis and continuous improvement team.

This one is a transportation company, it's a family business and used to be highly successful, and sadly it has fallen on hard times and currently doesn't make any money. It is based here in New York State but also has garages and depots in Canada and Mexico. These depots are largely but not exclusively leased by the company. This is a road transportation company and its vehicles run the gamut from tractor trailers to flatbed trucks to in-town delivery vans; the company owns all of the vehicles and has an excellent safety record. All of these vehicles are maintained in three in-house garages that are staffed by excellent class 'A' mechanics, the fleet is old but it's beautiful!

Unfortunately, the economic slowdown over the past few years has put the squeeze on the company, many of its customers have either closed down or are running at reduced output and the knock-on effect has resulted in reduced business and underutilization of the fleet and so the business barely breaks even.

Nonetheless, the company's reputation for quality, safety, and on-time delivery makes it a stand-out opportunity for anyone who is interested in transportation, and we most certainly are."

There's a whole lot of silence in the room from the senior execs and particularly from the chairman of the board.

"Our current business relies on transportation, almost exclusively road transportation, the only exception being the contact center division."

Lights are going on in people's heads all across the room.

"Although we own some of our trucks, the vast majority of them are leased and a great deal of our transportation is carried out by external transportation companies, all of our maintenance is outsourced. Our delivery routes take us all across North America, including Canada and Mexico of course. It would be our intent to service the metals, automotive, and the food and beverage company from our own internal transportation company."

The people in the audience are sitting forward, they seem to be already sold on the idea and yet Clive isn't finished.

"This same transportation company will continue to serve external customers, a great many of which are already on its roster, and of course it will also supply all the needs of our still-to-be-acquired pharmaceutical company and can company. Also, James mentioned international and big box, a well-run logistics company will cover all of these expectations too…we are going to have to grow this new transportation and logistics business of ours!"

Clive gets a standing ovation!

"Have you determined what it will cost us and who will run it?" asks Alex.

"Most of the vehicles and owned facilities are fully depreciated and so the price will be a fair one. The owner of the business would like to stay on and so the current plan proposes that he and I run it together; we will of course mesh our know-how and get our business improvement team involved to maximize the effectiveness and efficiency of the new business."

Clive sits down; he has every reason to be pleased with himself.

I'm on the floor again, "Next is a sweet little business, it's actually a chocolate company! Bill did most of the due diligence on this one with the help of Angela. I don't want to steal their thunder and so would ask them both to take the floor."

Bill and Angela step up. Bill is as usual wearing his serious face and Angela is beaming from ear to ear; when Bill meets her eye he has to fight to stop from grinning.

"You might wonder why we would be interested in something this size as initially so was I, however…as Rory says it's a very sweet deal; Angela, your thoughts please."

"Well, I have two bosses: Mr. Dent, who, as you know, heads up our food and beverage business, and the outrageous Rory McGregor, who needs no introduction. Both of them are fascinated with this opportunity and as I work in the retail side of our business, it seems I was a natural fit for the due diligence on this one, and this delights me!"

"It's a small business with ten retail stores strategically positioned across the United States with its flagship store in San Francisco, It also has an Internet presence," says Bill. "Its total sales are $5.0 million and it makes zero profit. The founder and owner takes a good salary, enough for a nice life, and that brings the entire business to break even. The cost breakdown for the business shows cost of goods at 40% wages at 30% and all other costs excluding the owner's salary run at 30%. The premises are all leased and the equipment is 100% depreciated. Tell us your thoughts, Angela."

"Well I don't want to spend your time explaining what you already know, so I'll get right to the point. Our food and beverage business is vertically integrated; we own a food processing plant and a packaging operation, which we utilize to produce our premium in-house product range. As you know, this line of products currently accounts for 40% of our total retail sales, and it carries the same price point as the top name brand products, which make up the remaining 60% of everything we sell in our retail stores; we are very proud of our in-house product and it has real cache.

In the early stages of our business analysis, Rory managed to intrigue us talking about what he refers to as the nut, a singular area of focus that is connected to all others around which we plan our control systems to maximize the business output. He gave examples that we could relate to in each of our divisions and they all set afire our imaginations; we've been using the concept across our company ever since. The example he gave that resonated with our food and beverage division was based on an experience he had more than a decade ago when he was charged with improving the top- and bottom-line performance of a chain of video stores; there are very few of those around today but back then all the big chains were still operating. This particular company had over three hundred outlets across a vast geography, the trick was to come up with a solution that could be installed and managed across the entire business...not easy!

Although the store management system had many elements, its core finally rested on the nut, which had two key measures: (1) the number of transactions per labor hour applied and (2) the dollar value of each transaction. It was found that small improvements in each of these two measures created an exponential improvement in the top line and even more so on the bottom line. Rory explained that many things have to change to achieve these results, but like most things in life they are completely doable. And that of course is one of the reasons why we love the chocolate company!"

"Back to you, Bill," says Angela.

"The deal is very attractive; we would keep the flagship store in San Francisco, move the rest of the business into our stores across the country while maintaining the chocolate company's look and feel, encourage their current employees to keep their jobs if they are prepared to move, reduce costs by eliminating the high lease costs of the premises we close, increase our Internet presence, use our buying power to reduce the cost of goods, and leverage the product line into our future geographic expansion, including the future big box business. The founder will stay with us; we will pay him fairly for his business and his ongoing support as chief content expert and chocolatier extraordinaire. There will also be an earnout available to him proportionate to the top line and profit growth of his product range. And we will most certainly utilize this new product line to arrive at the nut of more sales per available labor hour and more revenue per sale across our entire food and beverage company.

This is the same logic we will apply when making our new line of pharmaceutical products available through our existing stores and future big box stores; we will trigger natural product bundles with incentives to add them to the existing basket. We have other ideas on this concept currently in the works.

And so a relatively small but sweet deal has a projected 500% growth on the top line and a 30% bottom line in year one with lots more potential down the line."

Once again there is a lot of excitement in the room; we're all glad to see it as it will carry us a long way in the future.

"Finally, we have three opportunities to debrief: two are partnership based and could enhance our automotive business, one is based in Mexico and the other in China. The final opportunity this time around is in South Africa, it's an empty call center with no clients, but it is fully kitted out. It would be an asset buy within which we would place new and existing client business.

These opportunities touch on the very core of our strategy and values and so it is completely appropriate that James presents them."

This is a bit of a surprise to everyone in the room and everyone is highly attentive.

"Thanks Rory, I won't take up much of your time folks. So…all three of these opportunities would be quickly accretive to our business and add a higher EBIT than the average we are working toward, so you would think it likely that they would be an obvious yes.

You will recall that our strategy stresses fairness and concern for our employees and the communities in which we do business. I am in no way trying to judge how other people run their business, and yet I am intent that our ways represent our core belief structure.

Each of these business opportunities involves the benefits of labor arbitrage, lower wages than we pay our employees here in North America. I can only go along with that if we are progressive in our behavior and pay in the top ten percentile of the other businesses in the sector. We have gone into protracted negotiations on this as we believe the only good deal is one where everyone involved wins. The business in Mexico meets our criteria and the business in China currently does not. We will therefore monitor the business in China and encourage their ownership to improve the overall packages paid to their employees; we will pay a premium to encourage them to do this, but it's in the future!

The benefits of the automotive partnership will therefore include a reasonable degree of labor arbitrage, but it will also include a readymade plant skilled in producing subassemblies that our current customer base requires and which will be partially composed of products we ship from our existing facilities to Mexico, as everyone knows we have a free trade agreement with Mexico. Also our parts will be included in their subassemblies that they sell to their own current and future customer base; our joint intent is that our two companies will grow together to the benefit of both. There will be no job loss in our current business due to the partnership; in fact, we are planning for job growth.

Finally, the contact center opportunity in South Africa. All of the assets are top of the line, a few years old but completely serviceable, they will be fairly priced. The facility takes up two floors in a shopping mall, security is good and it is located at a road and rail transportation hub, which makes for easy commuting for our future employees. We know the quality, skill, and experience existing in the contact center community in this area, also the English is excellent. We know folks in Cape Town; we can hire the best management and through them everyone else. There are grants available for creating new jobs in the community, and so the only thing we need to make a go of it is customers!

We are already talking to our existing customer base and offering them a blended value solution, which they will find meets their business objectives, high value, and a healthy disaster recovery solution in case of any unexpected business interruption. Our intent is to take this on one floor at a time as we add new business.

And that, my friends, is the whole story."

Questions are taken and accolades are given; it is now in the hands of the CEO and the board of directors to decide on viability and agree the approach, and then negotiate pricing and timelines.

42

Two Years In

"Good morning, everyone. It's a great pleasure to welcome our employees at all levels of the business here today to this very special town hall meeting; everyone has been invited and the entire business has been closed down for two hours. Now of course everyone can't be in this room, we cover too much geography and have too many locations and too many people in our company to achieve that small miracle. As you are all aware though, we have booked cinema theaters everywhere we do business and right now our employees are tuned into a live broadcast event of this meeting. In fact, it could be said that those good folks got the best of the deal. Right now they are eating hot dogs, pizza, and popcorn with their soft drinks!"

The hall claps in acknowledgment at the good fortune of their colleagues.

"We, however, do have lots of folks from the shop floor here today along with the management team, lots of you gave up the popcorn to be here in this auditorium with your colleagues on the core acquisition due diligence and integration team. We are delighted to have the senior executives, leaders, and employees of the businesses we have merged with sitting here with us today also to share in what we believe is a celebration. It's been two full years since I approached the board with our thoughts and plans as to how we could grow our business...indeed double our business over a five-year period.

It's with pleasure that we are able to state that at this point in time we are slightly ahead of plan with run rate revenues of $1,850,000,000 for the last quarter against a target of $1,800,000,000 and an EBIT of 10.2% against a target of 10%. The success of our initiative to date is due to the dedication and good work of the people in this room as well as your colleagues who are unable to be here today due to their relaxing in comfy cinema chairs, all of them heroes.

I think it's appropriate for us to thank our board of directors for their support and commitment throughout this journey so far, we will not let them down in the future. You see...they represent all of you now! Their primary role is to take care of our shareholders, and thanks to our employee share plan you are indeed all shareholders of our company...and as you know it's in a meaningful way."

At this the entire room stands and gives a round of applause to the board of directors and to each other.

"We all thought it would be appropriate on this second annual review of our corporate strategy to take a little time to present to you what we believe are some of the key elements of our success so far. Members of the team, who all of you have come to know, will take part in this presentation, and as an aside it is interesting to note that all of the initial members of management are still present two years in, with the exception of Tony Dent, the president of our food division, who left us twelve months ago for what he considered was a better offer, we wish him well. With no further ado let me hand you over to your colleagues."

John, our COO, takes the floor, "Integrating a new business and maintaining a separate chain of command from the existing core business may have its attractions for our integration teams."

John pauses and looks around with a sardonic stare at Rory and the team.

"What?" says Rory "What?"

"Just kidding," says John. "You know I love you all to bits."

John continues, "The senior integration leader for each specific business unit has the freedom to avoid any potential politics and the seemingly endless report-outs. That lucky person would only have to concern themselves about their own little piece of the rock; we have taken on that model for our integrations and worked hard to give full authority and autonomy to the individual teams. And yet each part of the business relies on the other, just like all of us in this room rely on each other, in truth we are just one business, one team.

The performance of a business is in the sum of all its parts and it will seldom be smooth sailing everywhere at once. And so...things have to be pretty much constantly adjusted to achieve our overall goals.

It's interesting to listen to senior executive conversations when they are ruminating on business performance, very often they will disagree on the approach to running a business and yet more often than not they will agree that the overall performance tends to be a mixture of good guys or overperformance and bad guys...the underperformance from unexpected events and areas. Part of the executive's job is to steer the business through the smooth waters and also through the maelstroms, making the most of the good guys and minimizing the impact of the bad guys.

To make this work, everything has to be done in an integrated fashion, a holistic fashion.

Everything is a balancing act, a pinch more of this and an ounce less of that. It all tends to move along a continuum from roaring success to potential failure and all of the points in between.

The big picture approach to all of this may seem simple but the doing of it isn't necessarily easy, more like juggling with an orange, a feather, and a chain saw than a balancing act. Nonetheless, there has to be a big picture approach if we want to be able to manage the details where you stand, where we all stand! To achieve this, the plan includes the following elements:

- Plan involvement at all levels and locations.
- Have a strategic wide lens view of where we are going and when.
- Know where we currently are in relation to our desired strategic outcomes.
- Have a high level list of what must happen to close the gap between where we are now and where we want to be over time (critical issues).
- Ensure fair and reasonable responsibility and accountability is established for each of these critical issues.
- Establish the key drivers for each, the nut that we have to crack to optimize performance, and determine which levers have to be pulled to achieve the desired results that will move the needle in the desired direction.
- Determine the appropriate timelines of status updates in relation to the key measures at all levels and across the entire company.
- Ensure a high performance culture is in place, one that supports those responsible for results and yet holds all of us accountable.
- Ensure that there is a satisfying incentive program in place for everyone.
- Have a knowledgeable team available to go in and help when needed.
- Ensure that the performance system rewards both the expected performance and the desired behaviors.
- Adjust our aim, because we intend to do it all again and again.

We are going to go a little deeper into some of the above now; we want everyone in our company, everyone on our team to understand how we are really doing."

John hands the baton to our VP of human resources who will talk about the need to plan involvement at all levels, departments, and locations of the business.

"Hello, everyone, it's not my intention to come over as preaching here, and yet all of us seem to have acquired more than our share of zeal during the last two years. I've learned a lot, not least of all the need to get out from behind my desk and spend time with the folks who really do the work. Oh we all work and we all contribute, I know that and I'm not having a self-worth crisis here, but I'm not the person who handles one customer complaint call after another, or the person who applies the same weld to a frame hour after hour. These good folks, you good folks, need more than our support, you need our commitment and you have to know we care.

Taking the time to plan who we will involve in doing the work of our business goes a little further than just needing someone to help move your desk. If we are all going to be on the floor more, be closer to the action more, we will have to delegate some of the things we currently do by ourselves. So all of us must start thinking about it today, involve people wherever you can for their knowledge, their intelligence, their ideas, their creativity, their self-worth, their training...not just their good strong backs! You are our next supervisors, our next managers and it's our jobs to mentor you, to bring you on, just like it's everyone's job to help grow the person working next to them. Our stated intention in this company is to promote from within and so we should view everyone as our potential future boss. Give each other that degree of respect now and I can almost guarantee they will love you for it!

It's wise to remember that our newly acquired businesses will need a larger degree of nurturing in the early stages of being united with us than the business units that have always formed the core of our company. There is a likelihood that the employees in the acquired business may feel more insecure than we do, so we need to be there to spend time with those you are familiar with and those who are new to you. Take time every day; lend a hand when you can. If it's a call center sit with the agents and listen to calls with them, if it's a manufacturing process stand out on the production floor and watch and listen, introduce yourself and don't be a stranger. If it's the transportation business go out on the trucks, meet the customers and say hi, show interest everywhere and always follow through with any promises you make. If you're a manager, don't be a prisoner to your office or to a conference room; you can't be a real part of the business from behind closed doors.

Where does the time come from to be a real contributor to the business this way? Each of us gets 24 hours a day, no one gets 25, it's how we spend this time that matters. This truth holds good for everyone in the chain from senior executive through managers, supervisors, and individual performers; all of us are leaders with lots to offer. The objective for each of us is to do our job as best we can and to excel where we stand now. This in its perfect form can link up like a steel chain throughout the organization and it is the most likely way to achieve ongoing success.

It's more than a wish or a platitude to say that the most important asset in our business is our people, the commitment and performance of our people is golden, to deserve the best each of us has to be our best."

There's applause in the room and John is back on his feet, "Our CFO Billy has asked to be allowed to make the next presentation on having a strategic wide view of where the company is going and when."

"Hello everyone, thanks for giving me the opportunity of taking this time with you, our strategy is very close to my heart. If any of us are unsure of where the business is going and when, and for that matter what our part is in all of it we will always be waiting for something, and nature hates a vacuum and that's when fear might creep in.

The strategy that has been developed for our entire company must be communicated to everyone in such a way that their part in it is clear, the expected outcome for the division they work in, and the outcome for the team they work in. If there is any uncertainty then things have to be better explained, everyone must know the expectations for the outcome of their personal performance. It is all of our jobs to close the communication loop on this, to let everyone know how they are doing and not to have our people unsure of themselves. Never rely on folks having to make do with thinking that no news is good news. Each of us has a need to be informed, respected, and appreciated.

I'm sure everyone knows I'm the chief bean counter, so I would also like to take some time to explain the steps we have taken to tie our financial and strategic performance together, so that everything is truly integrated. I'll try not to be too dry!

When we develop a company strategy to guide us over a strategic time frame, which is normally for a period of three to five years, forward financial projections are stated for each of the years covered. These tend to indicate at a minimum, total sales dollars and EBIT dollars. Each year's budget will then be prepared in line with the strategy, and that strategy must of course go through a reality check every twelve months to ensure it is still valid. The budget is then broken down to reflect each of the four quarters of the current year, and eventually be reflected in a Profit and Loss account (P&L), which shows the revenue and cost and profit expectations of the company. The corporate P&L is then matched with the divisional expectations and broken down into monthly results, which again are projected into a divisional P&L. The actual performance of each division should be monitored in the shortest time frame possible to track the actual performance against the planned budget performance; any shortfall should be actioned immediately. The savvy company can identify proxies, units sold, calls handled, etc., that reflect the financial performance for the monthly budget and track these proxies on a daily basis thus giving an early warning of any shortfalls in our financials before the final accounting numbers are in. The sooner a shortfall is identified, the quicker it can be analyzed and actioned; this approach is at the heart of short interval reporting and speedy problem resolution. It is possible and desirable that the CEO and the divisional presidents should review these financial numbers on a one page document daily showing the performance of the previous day.

Formal update meetings will happen weekly, monthly, and quarterly whereas the informal analysis and problem solving can happen daily.

This same approach to tracking financial performance has been applied to the companies we have acquired, in this case the financial targets show a stretch that is connected to the targeted synergies. So short interval reporting is again a strategic imperative."

Bill takes his leave and John introduces Smithy to talk about the critical issues list:

"Where there are targets set that are in excess of previous performance it would seem obvious that they would simply not be achieved without deliberate action being taken, it's really not luck!

At the corporate level there will be a list of critical issues that have been developed to bridge the gap between our current performance and the future performance required during the strategic time frame, they will have been prioritized and sequenced against timelines with primary responsibility for each having been established and delegated.

At the divisional level there will be a list of opportunities developed from an ongoing analysis, which have also been prioritized and sequenced with the most logical person carrying the primary responsibility for the completion of each.

In the new acquisitions, the due diligence process will have unearthed opportunities and synergies that are also set against timelines for the realization of the gains they hold.

The achievement of these improvement streams, from corporate through division and into the newly acquired businesses must be synchronized with each other and then the results achieved to ensure the realization of the overall company performance targets. I am responsible as the head of the project management function to ensure these major initiatives are broken down into bite-sized chunks and then to ensure the monitoring of all of these pieces toward their successful conclusion."

Smithy sits down and Dave Mason, the president of our metals division, takes up the baton.

"I want to talk about responsibility and accountability; I'm personally responsible and accountable for a large piece of our overall business. It's not enough that the buck stops with me, it has to stop with everyone in the chain with each person being responsible and accountable for their own actions and output. The key to success in anything is accountability and if you're going to be accountable for something you must be given the responsibility and authority over it too.

The organizational chart should tell the whole story. In our case, I'm the division head for metals and I'm accountable for the performance of my direct reports who are made up of the senior people in every function of the division. It follows then that I am responsible for the entire division's performance as well as each of its component parts.

So how do we know if I am doing my job effectively? I am, only if the entire division and each of its component parts are achieving their planned business performance.

Next, each senior functional leader is responsible for the outputs and performance for their groups. Operations, Sales, Finance, IT, HR, etc. If for any reason any one of these functions does not meet its targeted performance, it will flag a potential failure in the entire company. If the functional leader cannot fix the problems then I have to step in.

This logic follows all the way through the chain of command all the way to the operators; each level of the organization should be equipped to perform their function and this includes enough working knowledge to support the people we are responsible for if needed, if we don't have enough working knowledge ourselves we must get help from either inside or outside the business.

The immediate performance level expected from an output is the responsibility of the person at the level at which it occurs; however, if there's a shortfall and if it's left unattended for too long, it becomes the responsibility of the next person up on the chain.

A bad situation left alone invariably gets worse, and remember we are it! We are all that we have!

There should be no surprises; everyone must have their finger on the pulse of the piece of the business they are responsible for. Management should be actively involved with their teams, seeing potential problems before they occur and actively working to eliminate actual problems that break through the surface of the business.

If we do this right with the help of short interval reporting, it will have the effect of the entire metals division functioning as one person, as strong as a steel chain through the entire organization with every link supporting the other."

Dave has clearly taken the improvement initiative to heart without losing any of his high standards of expectation!

"Each of our other three divisions run their business in this same way, as does the leaders of the businesses we acquired over the last two years. Standing at the head of all of the divisions is James, our CEO, and along with John and the other corporate executives he leads and manages our entire company using the same methods of responsibility and accountability as we do. Contrary to common belief, this can be achieved in harmony and fairness."

John introduces Tony, the top guy in our analysis team, who will talk about the need to establish the key drivers, including finding the nut at every major business intersection.

"Hi everyone, my name's Tony and my day job is in our automotive division, although during the past two years I've been seconded to the continuous improvement team working with Rory. If the CEO is forced to focus on every business metric across the company he or she will likely fail, and yet there is a need for the top person to know what is going on across the business in as near real time as possible. The last thing the CEO and for that matter the company needs is to be surprised by an irate client telling him his business is underperforming, and sadly this can happen if he is not up to speed and current. It follows that the right information must be presented to and discussed between the CEO and his direct reports daily. This fact holds true for all of us at every level of the organization.

The nut represents a small group of key measures that when combined represent the performance of the business or function under review, the sum of the parts must equal the whole.

Each nut must be constructed in such a way that it readily allows to bore down to the root cause of any problem and the necessary levers that must be pulled to get everything back on track. Each morning there should be a single page document on the CEO's desk and on those of his direct reports summing up the entire current performance of the business. It should always show the planned performance next to the actual performance achieved, these numbers should not be reviewed in a vacuum. Any shortfall should accompany a short paragraph of the actions that are being taken to resolve it.

By analyzing the key performance indicators daily, any problems, including where the departments and functions of the business intersect, will be apparent to everyone. Finance will show actual business performance to plan, Operations will show how well we are meeting demand for both quality and quantity, Sales will project future performance through current performance, Human resources will ensure that we are good employers and are up to date with recruiting, etc.

It is crucial that there is no fear at this or any other level of the business, if there is it will permeate all the way through. We don't rule by the sword, as well as making each other accountable we also support each other. If we can't do this, then number fudging will go on throughout the company, which will result in finger pointing, subpar performance, and unpleasant surprises.

Each senior functional head must replicate this approach with the nuts and levers modified to represent the outputs of their direct reports, and on down the line. Fifteen minutes maximum is the target for these reviews, we are not trying to create a make-work program. Follow-up meetings can and should be set where there are specific problems that require further input, discussion, and resolution."

John steps up to the front of the room and this time he's here to stay, "I think it's obvious that we find all this stuff fascinating and yet for us who don't have popcorn, things might be getting a bit boring, so we will finish up here. We hope this town hall meeting has been enlightening for everyone, and please know it's not a one shot deal; we will all get together every day at work and every year this way. All of us who took part in the actual presentations, although secretly we all think we are great orators, will fully understand if you choose the cinema option next time!"

43

Three Years In

The four division presidents and all of our new senior leaders from our acquired businesses are sitting together in the boardroom at head office. Alongside them are the senior department heads from across the entire business, plus John, Rory, Bill, Smithy, and me. The dynamic is very interesting; the atmosphere feels like there is no pressure at all and yet we are here to go over very important issues.

"Good to see you all," I say.

"Good to see you, James," echoes back at me in the most casual of fashions.

"It would be great today if we finished with our best go ahead ideas on the table," I say. "I mean, we're doing fine, pretty much on target for top- and bottom-line performance and everyone has good reason to be happy with that. I've just got this slight niggling feeling that this could all change in a heartbeat if we don't keep our focus on the road ahead. I feel we have to keep reinventing ourselves."

There's nods of agreement and comfortable responses made from around the table, not complacency, comfort in the thought that we will achieve something good today from our combined brain power.

Linda, our VP of sales and marketing, kicks in, "James, I think the elephant in the room is ensuring the ongoing growth of our top line while achieving our expected 12% EBIT; we've made strides in this direction and yet it feels like it's time for a new push."

John speaks up, "I think a lot of our bottom- and top-line gains have come from two sources. Oops, that's a pretty obvious statement, I'm just thinking out loud."

I nod to John, this is good. It's like a mastermind working here, all of our minds working together to get a superior output.

"What do you think, Rory?" I ask.

"I'm with John," Rory responds. "All the division presidents have their four-point plans in place to guide and manage the business in real time, the continuous improvement effort continues to yield real opportunities, and the synchronous process has created throughput opportunities for added sales right across the business."

Bill says, "Looking in the rear view mirror we look brilliant and yet the changes we have made just seemed to flow to us once our direction was clear. Our strategy is guiding us and our acquisitions are creating real synergies within themselves and as a part of the whole, building on top line and profit. We are well ahead of the curve."

Harry Wordsworth of the automotive group pipes up, "The companywide four-point planning updates are helping; they keep all of us on our game and allow us to apply resources to the right issues at the right time. I would never have believed that I personally would be so comfortable under the levels of scrutiny and transparency that the process affords us."

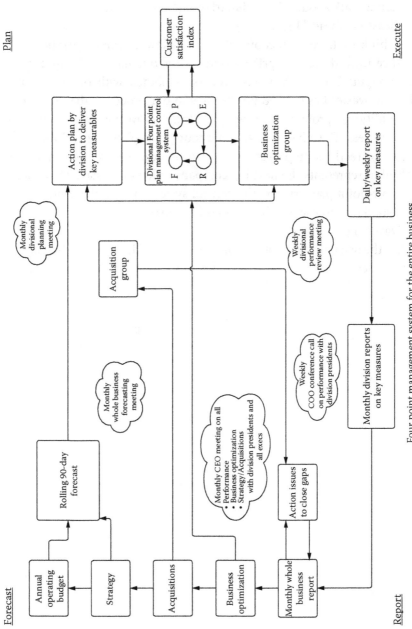

Plan

Execute

Forecast

Report

Four point management system for the entire business.

"I think it's the nonjudgmental approach that's making it work so well," says Helen of HR.

"Can we talk about sales and marketing?" asks Linda.

"Please go ahead," I say.

"I think we have been cooperating well between sales, operations, and finance to find creative pricing options for our increased capacity and throughput. The synchronous process combined with our eliminating the lean wastes has opened up the gaps in our processes that allow us to get additional profitable throughput. This has worked very well across the business. Dave has formalized a four-point planning technique that focuses directly on improved sales performance. We work on it as a team, I think it represents the next big companywide nut we have to crack and the four-point plan triggers the control system around that nut. It might be a good idea to use it right across the company."

"Dave?" I encourage.

"It's the usual thing, James," says Dave Mason. "It seems so obvious once it's in place.

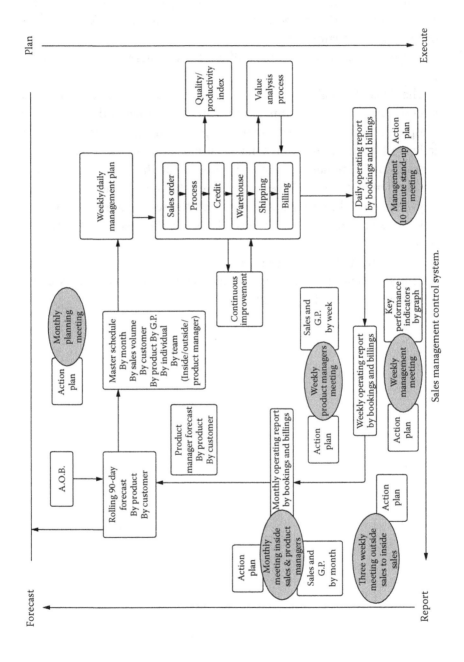

Sales management control system.

There is partnership participation between operations, sales, and finance with the goal of maximizing our sales opportunities. The control system simply works as triggers, performance checks, and feedback loops; does any of this sound familiar?"

Everyone is just nodding and smiling, there's interest but no surprises here.

"The elements speak for themselves, under the banners of forecast, plan, execute, and report. Our annual operating budget keeps the big picture of top- and bottom-line performance expectations in constant view. Our daily, weekly, and monthly plan makes sure we don't wander off track with our sales and materials inventory. The way you do the things you do…that was the Temptations I believe…god I loved that group when I was a kid. Anyway, we do things right and we check the results in short intervals, and we take the appropriate actions. The whole thing helps with peace of mind!"

"How do we all feel about this?" I ask.

Clearly everyone likes it. "I'll get to it and help install the process across the business with the help of Billy and Dave," says Linda.

44

Four Years In

I'm meeting with our chairman of the board in our favorite restaurant, "And how are you this evening, Alex?" I ask as we shake hands.

"All the better for your company, James; what surprises do you have in store for me tonight?"

"It's just an informal update before the board meeting, Alex, and how better to do it than while we sup on Beppi's spaghetti Bolognese?"

"I'm fascinated to hear what you have, James."

I produce a piece of clipart from my briefcase, "I've adapted this little diagram to show you where we are now and where we would like to go."

The seven pillars.

"We have built the new company on these seven pillars:

1. Strategy
2. Acquisitions
3. Business optimization
4. Continuous improvement
5. Company culture
6. Rewards and recognition for all our employees
7. Strong financial performance"

"I know you are happy with the results so far…we all are, and I'm pleased to report that we expect to meet all of our financial targets as a minimum by the close of year five."

Alex is studying the diagram, "Sort of like the seven pillars of wisdom James eh? Only with some elements of the Parthenon built on top!"

"The pieces on top, which are of course supported by the seven pillars, represent where we would like to go next. As you know we came in well below $1.0 billion for the costs of all our acquisitions combined and so with the blessings of the board we would like to invest a little more."

"Please go ahead, James."

"We have created extra throughput in all of our businesses and with all of our fixed costs taken care of we can come up with some very creative pricing, as you know we have already done this with existing and new clients inside our current divisions. What you see represents new green field opportunities for us, some of which are partnerships."

"I'm intrigued, James, please continue."

"It's all really quite simple and any costs will still leave us well under the $1 billion we originally planned, I'll talk you through them one at a time."

- We would like to get into a partnership with one of the big box outlets that operate in Canada and the United States. We will make the preliminary approach through our broker if and when the board agrees it. The idea would be to supply them with our name brand food and beverage products and pharmaceuticals, not to mention Willy's Wonderful Chocolates. We will of course use our own high-speed packaging operation for the food and beverages we sell and part of the deal would also wrap in our transportation company.
- We would also like to supply grocery stores all across North America with our name brand products, the same for pharmacies. Once again

this will benefit the same aspects of our business as those that support the big box partnerships.
- We also want to make a separate logistics division that will supply metals to metal supermarket outlets.
- It looks as though it might be the right time to do the partnership deal with the Chinese automotive parts manufacturer, so we will ask for the go ahead on that one too.
- Lastly, we will formalize our own consulting business as a partnership between us and Rory, this won't cost us anything, it's actually a profit center and half of its current work is already from outside our company with our customers and suppliers. It's growing like a weed and the external work generates a full 33% profit. The prices charged to our internal businesses are nominal and will always receive the priority.

"Do you think this will keep Rory with us?" asks Alex.

"Yes I do."

"All right," says Alex, "I'll take it to the board; anything else?"

"No, I think that covers it for now, Alex."

"Ok then, let's enjoy dinner. Oh…and by the way, did I thank you for everything you're doing?"

"Yes you did, Alex…thank you."

45

Five Years In

James is just finishing up his presentation to the board of directors and they are happy, and so they should be! Every target has been hit as we approach the five year mark from the beginning of the business expansion and its optimization, it wasn't always easy, but then how could it have been? We've virtually doubled the top line sales of the company and increased the overall EBIT by 50%.

"Well...we have given you the state of the nation, how we are running our company and how we feel it needs to be run into the future. Also how we believe we must integrate any new acquisitions we make into our existing core business. We've done our best to be as prescriptive as possible and yet it is possible that our briefing has left you with some questions. So this is an opportunity for those questions to be asked and hopefully answered to everyone's satisfaction. You'll note we haven't changed the seating and so there is no moderator and no panel, all of our team is present, anyone can ask questions and anyone can answer them. If there's need for debate, then we will debate."

James settles down and the questions begin, tentatively at first and then with a great surge.

Question: How do you explain the extraordinary success of this five year journey?

Answer: We planned ahead, involved all of our people, used the right tools, and took the right steps at the right time. We then followed up relentlessly and never accepted the thought of failure.

Question: What makes us believe we can achieve all the synergies we have identified going into the future?

Answer: We might not achieve all of them, but we will pick up the slack from other opportunities if we miss any of the original targeted synergies.

Question: How do you know that?

Answer: Because we've done it before; every P&L and every cost saving opportunity has had their hits and misses. We are prepared for that and are always looking for the next best opportunity, we have to start somewhere and our starting points are always well thought out in advance.

Question: How did we determine the growth strategies for top line and profit performance in the core business and in the acquisitions...was it SWAG? A strategic wild ass guess?

Answer: No...not a SWAG, I'm not saying we are not capable of starting with a SWAG though!

Lots of laughter in the room.

We looked at best practices and the best in class companies across the industries we operate in and we used their performance as our guidelines. We verified all of this, as most of you well know, with in-depth analysis. The same holds true for the companies we targeted for acquisitions.

Again as most of you know, the acquisitions tend to support our current core businesses as well as each other, and this has allowed for quantum leaps in growth and profit improvement. It's finding these one off "good guys" that allows us a little breathing room in achieving our overall targeted goals.

Question: What if it all goes wrong? What if we fail? Will there be a witch hunt?

Answer: No...I'm pleased to state that the witch hunting days ended at Salem. I'm responsible, the buck stops here, every acquisition, every improvement, and every change in how we do business has my signature to it. Our team is the best, they have proven it by their results over the last five years; going forward it's me and the rest of the company executive that has to keep up with this brilliant team, and we will!

Question: How can you be so confident when most companies who attempt this degree of expansion fail?

Answer: There's no room for lack of confidence in business or for that matter in life. You use the best brainpower that's available, you validate your ideas and proposals, and you go ahead when you're confident that it's the most prudent and the best path to do so.

Question: What then?

Answer: You commit and you follow through; more than a century ago Andrew Carnegie said "Put all of your eggs in one basket, and then watch the basket!" We have watched the basket and we will be watching the basket going forward, constantly performing checks and balances and redirecting our aim where appropriate.

Question: How can we be like you, so sure, so confident?

Answer: We need your continued support and we will earn it. We will never leave you in the dark; we have the actual performance results of the company at our finger tips daily and we will continue to share them with you in a timely fashion.

Question: Going forward, how can we expect the people in the companies we acquire to be confident, won't they be afraid for their jobs?

Answer: Yes, some of them will be afraid for their jobs and some may well lose their jobs. When we let people go we will be fair and honorable and we will be seen to be fair and honorable. As indeed we have been with the companies we have already acquired over these past five years. From the get go we will involve everyone in the running of the business, the acquired companies' leaders are sitting with our original leadership team here at this meeting, and for that matter at every meeting, everyone's input is equally valid. We must always remember we are a growth story and not a contraction story, as long as we get this right we will be creating jobs not divesting them.

Question: So...when we complete this next round of acquisitions and get them integrated, and get our current business optimized...are we finished?

Answer: Absolutely not! Standing still in any business is not an alternative; if we stand still we will be left behind. We've completed the first five years from the outset of this change process and we are looking forward to the next five, so we will buckle up and continue to achieve all the targets we've set for ourselves into the future.

Question: What will stop performance from slipping, what will keep us fresh and on the ball?

Answer: You will! I will! He will! She will! Every leader in our business will, and truly everyone in our business is a leader and we have to make sure everyone is treated that way. A person might be working on the line today, but they might well be my boss tomorrow!

And then there's Rory and his team; they are going to be a permanent feature in our lives. They will conduct wellness audits on all aspects of our company every year, and they will ensure we are not getting ourselves off course. We now have our own internal consulting company and it will prove to be a parallel path for our folks to advance their careers through the company, two interlinking paths, leadership and continuous improvement.

There are no further questions and so we all stop for a chat, a muffin and a cup of coffee, and to talk one on one about the future; this conversation goes on between the members of the board and our employees throughout the room; nobody seems to want to leave!

After the meeting has broken up and we have escorted our guests to their cars, John, Rory, and I head to our sanctuary at the entrance to our office, Joe's coffee shop. We settle down at a table and Joe wanders over, "Late start today, boys?" he asks.

John gives Joe his usual sardonic look, but for just a moment he seems completely lost for words.

Joe shrugs and asks his question, "The usual?" We nod and he wanders off.

"It's been good guys," I say. "Are both of you going to hang in there for the next ride?"

"Are you hanging in, James?" asks John.

"Yes, I'm a lifer; Martha and I went to see a show last night, you remember the Temptations? Anyway there's only one of the originals left now and he's been with the group for fifty-five years! I like that!"

"Then I'll be staying too," says John. "I can't promise that I'll last for fifty-five years but I'll commit to the next five and we'll see where we go from there."

"What about you, Rory?" I ask. "We took advantage of your loyalty to drag you back from retirement; we won't hold it against you if you head back to Morocco."

Rory nods, "I think I owe it to Betsy to take things a bit easier," he says looking over his shoulder. "Oh good grief James, did I leave Betsy at your house with Martha?"

"So are you leaving?" asks John with disbelief and no sign of approval whatsoever.

"We have a good team with trained and good systems in place; our boys and girls can run things. So I'll drop to half time if that's ok with you guys."

"You'll come when I need you?" I ask.

"Of course," says Rory, "Just like the Temptations."

"So we've done a lot of things here together guys, if you had to pick the one that has stood out as the foundation of our success over the past five years what would it be."

John and Rory look at each other and answer pretty much in unison, "That would be our culture, James; it can be embodied in the three-legged stool, equal respect and focus to our three main constituents, our customers, our employees, and our shareholders. Anyone who looks at our company can easily see that's how we function. As long as our top three constituents are happy and know their needs are respected we're going to have a happy and successful company."

James nods his agreement and with no apparent show of emotion says, "All right guys, let's get back to work," and he rises to leave the table. "Oh… by the way…did I say thanks for the brilliant job you have done?"

"You did, James," we respond, "thank you very much."

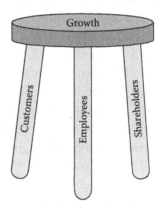

The three-legged stool.

The "Grow or Die" Ultimatum: Creating Value through Acquisitions and Blended Long-Term Improvement Formulas.

Companies often grow through acquisition; it is quick and if properly done it is also effective. But why is it that 95% of acquisitions fail to achieve the targeted synergies that triggered them in the first place?

The truth is that Mergers and Acquisitions are bloody hard work, and you can't expect to get better just by getting bigger!

It is asking for trouble if we see acquisitions as the panacea, the cure to growing a business that is not currently performing. In the early days of business automation, it was clearly understood that a production line must work effectively in the manual mode before it was automated. This same truth holds good for entire companies; they must run effectively as they stand before we build upon them through acquisition. These same tools that we use in the preparatory phase of the process while optimizing our current business, including Lean, Six Sigma, and Theory of Constraints, become the catalyst that will maximize business growth, cash flow, and net profits for the business in the long term. They are transferrable and form an integral part of "the glue" that holds the newly acquired company and the core business together.

The "Grow or Die" Ultimatum: Creating Value through Acquisitions and Blended Long-Term Improvement Formulas

This uses a compelling story format through a collection of stories that illustrate best practices for making acquisitions work while optimizing your current business. It uses in-depth case studies to illustrate a range of scenarios at a business process outsourcer; automotive parts manufacturer, metals distributor, and a food and beverage company.

Readers will learn how a mid-sized company can protect itself against the probable costs of a failed acquisition by following a gated approach in progressing from one step to the next.

How to ensure the targeted acquisitions offer very real synergies to the acquiring company through the conducting of in-depth due diligence and effective integration. Parallel to this is the optimizing of overall business performance through the effective utilization of existing resources by involving and mobilizing the workforce through effective communication and training. Readers will better understand the complexities in newly formed working relationships, as well as how to

- Hire and work with consultants
- Interact with management to get things done
- Engage workers on the front line
- Build and sustain a high performance culture

The book includes coverage of strategic planning, project planning, four-point planning, due diligence, business integration, theory of constraints, managing the performance system, command and control, root cause analysis, and finance.

Index

About the Author

My working career began as a tool-and-die maker and as a marine engineer in Scotland. No university for me—I maxed out with a college degree in engineering. I had no choice but to succeed!

I progressed through supervisory roles with Chrysler Corporation and then management roles with American Can International in the United Kingdom and North America. My first consulting role was with Kepner Tregoe and Associates, a company with a reputation as a gold standard in rational thinking processes.

Ever the reader, I was triggered into fashioning myself as half-executive and half-consultant. As an executive I rose over the years to become the chief operating officer with Minacs Worldwide and as managing director with Teletech Australia and New Zealand. I have managed profit and loss responsibility on five continents. As a consultant, I have been engaged in business turnaround in the automotive parts, metals distribution, and BPO sectors.

My grassroots beginnings and the length of my career have given me experience and expertise in business process outsourcing, call centers, automotive parts manufacturing, metals distribution and processing, plastics, the pharmaceutical and food and beverage industries, and high-speed packaging.

I am the coauthor with my brother Steven of *The Success or Die Ultimatum: Saving Companies with Blended Long-Term Improvement Formulas* (CRC Press, Taylor & Francis Group, 2015).

I am also the founder and principal of Daniel Borris & Associates Ltd., a Canada based management consulting firm, and can be reached at danielborris@yahoo.ca.

Daniel Borris